GCSE English

To Kill a Mockingbird

by Harper Lee

Studying English texts can give you a real headache,
but happily this CGP book makes your life just a little bit easier.

This book has everything you need to write a brilliant essay about *To Kill a Mockingbird*. It doesn't just tell you what happens — it's got analysis of the main characters, themes, historical background and language features too.

Plus, there are plenty of practice questions and a worked exam answer with tips on how to improve your grade on the big day.

And of course, we've done our best to make the whole experience at least vaguely entertaining for you.

The Text Guide

Contents

Introduction

Section One — Background and Context

Section Two — Discussion of Chapters

Section Three — Characters

Contents

Section Four — Themes

Section Five — The Writer's Techniques

Section Six — Exam Advice

Published by CGP

Editors:
Rachael Powers
Holly Poynton

Contributors:
Jane Harrison
Elisabeth Sanderson

With thanks to Paula Barnett and Glenn Rogers for the proofreading.

Acknowledgements:

Cover Illustration by Raphael Capalad © 2011

With thanks to Rex Features for permission to use the images on pages 7, 21, 49, 50 & 55

Images on pages 5, 18, 24, 35, 47, 52 & 56 © UNIVERSAL / THE KOBAL COLLECTION

Photographs on pages 5, 6, 7, 20, 23, 27, 31, 32, 33, 40, 41, 42, 43, 51, 57, 58 & 59 © copyright 2007 Leigh Toldi Photographs are from the San Mateo High School production of "To Kill a Mockingbird", directed by Brad Friedman, May, 2007, San Mateo, California.

With thanks to Getty Images for permission to use the images on pages 3 & 11

With thanks to Mary Evans Picture Library for permission to use the images on pages 4 & 8

With thanks to Alamy for permission to use the images on pages 9 & 10

Thanks to The Touring Consortium Theatre Company (www.touringconsortium.com) for permission to use the images on pages 5, 6, 14, 19, 29, 30, 34, 37, 38, 39 & 46 © Karl Andre Photography Limited

With thanks to The Moviestore Collection for permission to use the images on pages 7, 15, 16, 17, 28 & 36

ISBN: 978 1 84762 023 1

Printed by Elanders Ltd, Newcastle upon Tyne.

Clipart from Corel®

Based on the classic CGP style created by Richard Parsons.

Introducing 'To Kill a Mockingbird' and Harper Lee

'To Kill a Mockingbird' is about the dangers of prejudice

- *To Kill a Mockingbird* is about the trial of a black man who's been falsely accused of raping a white woman.
- Although it's fictional, it's based on real attitudes towards black people in 1930s Alabama and real events like the Scottsboro Trials.

The Scottsboro Trials

1) The Scottsboro Trials happened in Alabama, beginning in 1931 — nine black men were accused of raping two white women.
2) Even though there was medical evidence that proved the women hadn't been raped, the all-white jury sentenced all the men except the youngest to death. The men were also nearly lynched before the trial.
3) Some of the men served prison time but after several re-trials almost all of them were freed.

Harper Lee believed in equality

- Harper Lee wrote *To Kill a Mockingbird* during the Civil Rights Movement in the late 1950s when people were campaigning for black people to have equal rights to white people.
- She wanted to show that racism is unfair.

1926	Born in Monroeville, Alabama as Nelle Harper Lee.
1945	Starts a law course at the University of Alabama.
1949	Drops out of university to move to New York and concentrate on writing.
1956	Friends give Lee enough money to fund her writing career for a year.
1960	'To Kill a Mockingbird' is published.
1961	'To Kill a Mockingbird' wins the Pulitzer Prize.
1962	'To Kill a Mockingbird' is made into a film starring Gregory Peck as Atticus.
2010	'To Kill a Mockingbird' has sold an estimated 30 million copies worldwide.

Background Information

'To Kill a Mockingbird' is set in Maycomb, Alabama

Maycomb is a fictional place, but it's based on the town of Monroeville in Alabama where Harper Lee grew up. Here are the key locations in the novel:

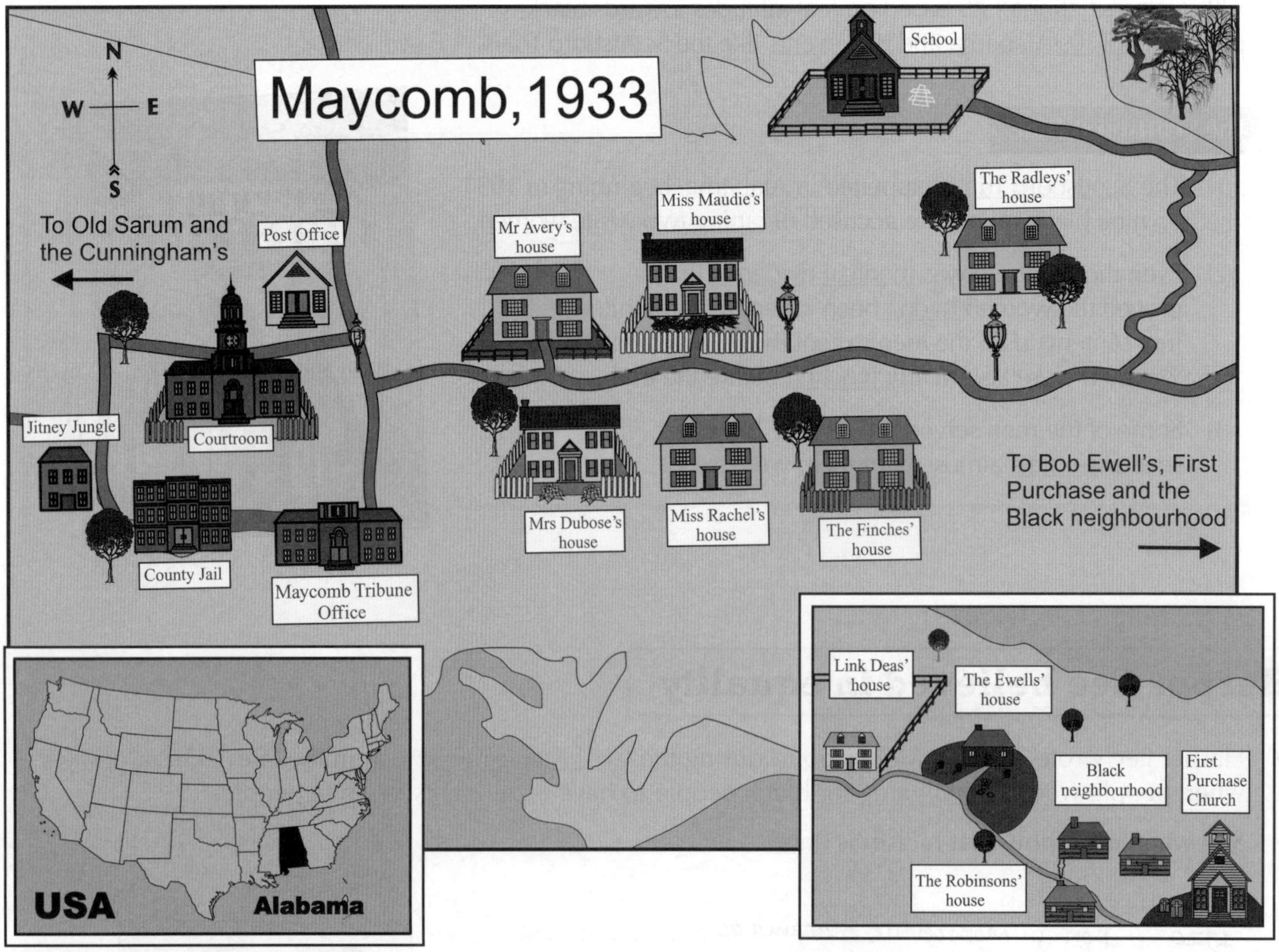

Maycomb, 1933
N
W
E
S
School
To Old Sarum and the Cunningham's
Post Office
Mr Avery's house
Miss Maudie's house
The Radleys' house
Jitney Jungle
Courtroom
County Jail
Maycomb Tribune Office
Mrs Dubose's house
Miss Rachel's house
The Finches' house
To Bob Ewell's, First Purchase and the Black neighbourhood
USA
Alabama
Link Deas' house
The Ewells' house
Black neighbourhood
First Purchase Church
The Robinsons' house

Life in 1930s America was tough

- In 1865 slavery was abolished in the USA. Hundreds of Southern businesses now had to employ paid staff to replace their unpaid slaves, so their profits suffered.
- In 1929 the American stock market collapsed. Thousands of people lost their jobs and many couldn't make enough to earn a living.
- The Southern states were hit hard by the collapse of the stock market because crop prices fell and the Southern economy was still recovering from the abolition of slavery.
- The period between 1929 and the late 1930s was known as the Great Depression. People were very poor and they wanted to blame someone for their poverty — people of different races were an easy target.

Families queue for food during the Great Depression.

Who's Who in Maycomb

Photograph by Leigh Toldi

Scout Finch...

...is the narrator of the novel. She's a stubborn tomboy who's always getting into trouble.

Photograph by Leigh Toldi

Jem Finch...

...is Scout's older brother. He sometimes teases his sister but he takes good care of her.

© Karl Andre Photography Limited

Atticus Finch...

...is Scout and Jem's father. He's a lawyer and teaches the children a lot about respect.

Photograph by Leigh Toldi

Dill...

...visits Maycomb every summer and is friends with Jem and Scout.

Photograph by Leigh Toldi

Calpurnia...

...is the Finches' housekeeper. She doesn't take any nonsense from the children but looks after them well.

Photograph by Leigh Toldi

Aunt Alexandra...

...is Atticus's sister. She's stern and snobbish but she gets on well with the other Maycomb ladies.

Tom Robinson...

...is a local man accused of raping Mayella. He's compassionate and hardworking.

Photograph by Leigh Toldi

Boo Radley...

... is a mysterious man who lives down the road from the Finches. He's the victim of local gossip.

© UNIVERSAL / THE KOBAL COLLECTION

Photograph by Leigh Toldi

Bob Ewell...

...is an abusive father who lives by a dump. He's racist and rude.

Photograph by Leigh Toldi

Mayella Ewell...

...is Bob's daughter. She claims she was raped by Tom. She has a hard home life — she has to look after her seven younger siblings and her father beats her.

'To Kill A Mockingbird' — Plot Summary

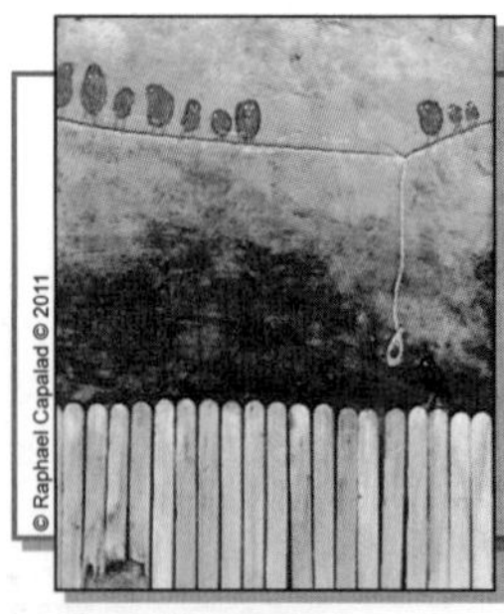
© Raphael Capalad © 2011

'To Kill a Mockingbird'... what happens when?

Here's a little recap of the main events of *To Kill a Mockingbird*. It's a good idea to learn what happens when, so that you know exactly how the plot progresses and how all the important events fit together.

Chapters One to Eight — setting the scene

Photograph by Leigh Toldi

- The reader is introduced to the story's narrator Scout and her brother Jem, their father Atticus and their friend Dill who visits every summer.
- Scout starts school. She doesn't get on with her teacher, Miss Caroline.
- The children try to persuade Boo Radley to come out of his house.
- Mysterious gifts start to appear in the tree outside the Radley House.
- Snow falls in Maycomb for the first time in years and Miss Maudie's house burns down.

Chapters Nine to Fifteen — the children learn some lessons

- Scout and Jem find out that Atticus has been asked to defend a black man accused of raping a white woman.
- Atticus kills a mad dog.
- Mrs Dubose insults Atticus and Jem chops the heads off all her flowers. Atticus makes Jem go and read to Mrs Dubose every day as a punishment.
- Mrs Dubose dies and it turns out the reason she was so unpleasant was because she was weaning herself off morphine.
- Calpurnia takes the children to the black people's church. Most people are nice to them but one woman is prejudiced against them because they're white.
- Aunt Alexandra comes to live with the Finches and tries to turn Scout into a lady.
- Dill turns up at the Finches' house — he's run away from home.
- A lynch mob threatens to attack Atticus outside the county jail, but Scout stops them.

Chapters Sixteen to Twenty-Three — the trial

- Tom Robinson's trial begins.
- The Ewells testify first — Bob's rude and obnoxious and Mayella thinks Atticus is teasing her when he talks to her politely.
- Tom Robinson comes to the stand. He tells the court that Mayella asked him to come inside her house and tried to kiss him. He says he ran away when Bob Ewell turned up.
- Atticus points out that Mayella's injuries happened on the right side of her face — suggesting that she was attacked by someone left-handed. Bob Ewell is left-handed but Tom Robinson's left arm is completely useless.

Photograph by Leigh Toldi

- Despite Atticus proving that Tom couldn't have caused Mayella's injuries, the jury finds him guilty.
- The black people at the trial stand up when Atticus leaves the courtroom out of respect, but the children are upset and disappointed by the unfairness of the verdict.

Chapters Twenty-Four to Thirty-One — the attack

© Moviestore Collection Ltd

- Scout has tea with Aunt Alexandra and the missionary ladies, who want to help the black Mruna tribe in Africa.
- Tom Robinson is killed trying to escape from prison.
- Bob Ewell breaks into Judge Taylor's house and starts following Tom's wife Helen.
- Scout and Jem take part in a Halloween pageant and someone attacks them on their way home.
- Boo Radley saves the children from their attacker and carries Jem home.
- Heck Tate tells Atticus that it was Bob Ewell who attacked the children and that he died during the attack.
- He convinces Atticus that Bob's death was accidental and that it would be a "sin" to accuse Boo of having a role in Bob's death.
- Scout walks Boo home and reflects on what she has learnt.

Now you've got into the swing of things...

... there's lots to learn. Once you're confident you know what happens in *To Kill a Mockingbird*, turn over the page to start Section One, which is all about the historical context of the novel. If you're still unsure about the novel's plot or want a break from revision, have a look at the *To Kill a Mockingbird* cartoon at the back of the book.

© Everett Collection/Rex Features

The American South

You need to know a bit about the history of the South to really understand *To Kill a Mockingbird*. The events of the 19th century shaped the attitudes of the characters in 1930s Maycomb.

The story really begins with the slave trade

1) The slave trade brought millions of Africans to work in America. Slaves were brought across in slave ships and suffered terrible conditions, both on the journey and once they arrived.
2) Slaves had no rights — they were bought by wealthy white people and then forced to work in the fields or mines. They couldn't leave their jobs, and had no say in what happened to them.
3) Slavery wasn't abolished in America until 1865, and by then the idea that black people were inferior was the norm in many places.

Slaves being taken from their homes and forced onto a slave ship

Slavery played a big part in the Civil War (1861–1865)

1) The American Civil War was between the Northern United States and eleven Southern states called the Confederate States of America.
2) The civil war was violent and bloody — around 620 000 soldiers died.
3) One of its main causes was disagreement over slavery — those in the North wanted to abolish it whereas those in the South wanted to keep it. Slavery was abolished in 1865 — because the Northern states overwhelmed the Southern states in the end.
4) Even after the abolition of slavery, attitudes towards black people took a long time to change. In Maycomb, black people don't have the same rights or opportunities that the white people have — they aren't entitled to an education and can only get poorly paid jobs like cotton picking.

Theme — Family

Scout's cousin Ike Finch is described as the county's only surviving Confederate veteran, which means the war between the Northern and Southern states is still remembered by some.

The Ku Klux Klan was a group of white extremists

Theme — Intolerance

Atticus tells Jem the Klan will "never come back". However, although the Ku Klux Klan had lost most of their power by the 1930s, the actions of the mob outside the county jail suggests that violence towards black people is still a very real threat.

1) The Ku Klux Klan was formed in the 1860s by a group of white men who'd fought for the Confederate States of America. The Klan believed that white people were superior to everyone else.
2) They would attack and kill black Americans, as well as white Americans who'd been on the Northern states' side.
3) In the early 1920s there was an estimated 4 million members of the Ku Klux Klan living in the South, but these numbers had dropped by the 1930s.

The American South

The town of Maycomb is representative of the kind of places where people lived in the South in the 1930s. But Maycomb just makes me think of hairbrushes you can only use for one month a year...

This history pops up everywhere in the novel

1) The history of the Finch family is linked to the history of the South — their ancestor Simon Finch had three slaves who helped him to build the family home. Until Atticus went to law school the family made its living by farming cotton.
2) Cotton was the major crop in the South and slaves were often used to harvest it.
3) People are proud of the area's history and of their family histories — Scout tells us the Finch family are Southerners on the first page of the novel.

Workers picking cotton in the American South

There are lots of references in the novel to history and what it means to be a Southerner — this reminds you that people's views will be difficult to change because the past is still really important to them.

Maycomb isn't a real place

Maycomb is a fictional place but it could be any Southern town. A lot of the characters and events help the reader to see what life was really like in Alabama in the 1930s.

The layout of the town is described in detail and the characters are familiar townspeople — doctors, lawyers, maids, school children etc.

Harper Lee wants Maycomb to be recognisable to show that prejudice can happen in any Southern American town.

There are a lot of prejudiced characters in the book, but even the prejudiced characters almost always have good qualities too.

This shows how even likeable people often have prejudices — for many people racism was a normal part of everyday life.

Nothing much ever changes — even snow is really rare.

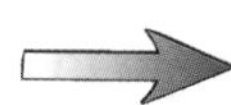

This shows the town is stuck in its ways — it'll take ages to change people's attitudes.

Mention the importance of the novel's historical context...

The events of the 19th century have a big influence on the issue of race in *To Kill a Mockingbird* — if you can link historical events to things that happen in the novel, the examiner will be seriously impressed.

1930s America

The book is set during the Great Depression, which is about as fun as it sounds. Why don't historians give these things more light-hearted names like the Great Kitten Era or the Tasty Cake Generation?

1930s America was not a very happy place to be

1) In 1929, the American stock market collapsed. This was called the Wall Street Crash and it caused a global financial downturn known as the 'Great Depression'.
2) The Depression in America didn't just affect people who worked on the stock market. It also affected crop prices and reduced demand for products such as coal and wood.
3) People couldn't earn a living — the average American income dropped by 40% between 1929 and 1932. Loads of people left their homes in search of work.

Roosevelt tried to improve things with his New Deal

1) Franklin D Roosevelt was elected President of the United States of America in November 1932.
2) He introduced his 'New Deal' — a number of government programmes to help America recover.
3) Under Roosevelt's leadership the economy did begin to recover, but progress was slow.
4) Roosevelt's New Deal created new optimism and people's lives were improving. But people suffered a lot during the Depression, particularly farmers in the South because the Southern economy was still trying to recover from the abolition of slavery.

The aims of the New Deal were:

Relief — giving people financial help.

Recovery — rebuilding US industry and trade.

Reform — changing conditions to ensure progress.

The Great Depression affected Maycomb

1) This depression is what Atticus is talking about when he mentions that times are hard for people. There's a lot of poverty in the book. Even the Finches aren't wealthy — Scout says that "nickels and dimes were hard to come by".
2) Some families, like the Cunninghams, were hit especially hard. In chapter 2, Atticus explains that a lot of families faced tough decisions. Mr Cunningham could get a welfare job but it would mean letting his farm go to ruin.
3) Bob Ewell is another character affected by the Great Depression. He's given "relief checks" by the government to help feed his family.
4) The Great Depression helps to explain why some people were so racist in Maycomb — a lot of land owners like the Cunninghams blamed the end of slavery for loss of profits, land and status.

An unemployed man selling apples to make money during the Depression

1930s America

Unfortunately, things aren't much cheerier on this page. In fact it's pretty distressing stuff, but you've got to know just how bad racism was in the 1930s to fully understand Maycomb's prejudice.

American society was racist in the 1930s

1) In 1930s America, it was normal for white and black people to be segregated (kept apart). In the South, a black man could risk being lynched (murdered by a mob) if he so much as looked at a white woman.
2) Between 1889 and 1930, around 3700 people were lynched in America. It wasn't just black people who were killed — white people could be lynched for sympathising with black people.
3) In 1930, two young black men called Thomas Shipp and Abram Smith were lynched. They had been accused of rape and murder — but not tried or convicted. A crowd broke into the jail where they were being held, and killed them.

The lynching of Thomas Shipp and Abram Smith in 1930.

But things were beginning to change by the 1950s

1) By the early 1950s things hadn't really improved for black people — they were still denied basic human rights.
2) But in the mid-1950s things began to change — black activists like Martin Luther King began a series of peaceful protests like bus boycotts, sit-ins and marches. This campaign for equality was known as the Civil Rights Movement.
3) Although some white people supported the Civil Rights Movement, there were some people — particularly in the South — who still thought black people were inferior.
4) When Harper Lee wrote *To Kill a Mockingbird* in the late 1950s the Civil Rights Movement was in full swing — her novel captured the mood of the time because it gave hope for the future.

Theme — Intolerance

Atticus tells Jem and Scout that white people are "going to pay the bill" for their treatment of black people. This is an example of dramatic irony — when the book was published black Americans were campaigning for equality.

Dramatic irony is when the reader realises the significance of what a character says or does before the other characters.

Show how intolerance in the novel is linked to its context...

Lee doesn't exaggerate the racism in the novel — it was all there in 1930s America. If it's relevant, you could earn some marks in the exam by comparing the treatment of Tom Robinson to Shipp and Smith.

Practice Questions

It certainly wasn't a very cheerful time to write a novel about, what with the Depression and people being oppressed all over the place. You have to admire Harper Lee for doing such a good job of lightening things up a bit. Despite all the sad bits, 'To Kill a Mockingbird' isn't a gloomy book. It's funny, moving and uplifting and I bet you're sick of the sight of it. Well, tough. Get on with these questions.

Quick Questions

1) In what year was slavery abolished in America?

2) What was one of the main causes of the American Civil War?

3) Who were the original Ku Klux Klan?
   a) a group of soldiers who fought for the Confederate States of America
   b) a group of soldiers who fought for the Northern United States
   c) the Cunninghams

4) Why does Harper Lee describe the layout of Maycomb in such detail?

5) What was the Great Depression?

6) Which American President introduced the New Deal?

7) What does 'segregation' mean?

8) What does 'lynching' mean?

9) Roughly how many people were lynched in America between 1889 and 1930?

10) What was the Civil Rights Movement?

Practice Questions

This, you'll be pleased to know, is the very first set of In-depth Questions in the book. Write some beautiful answers to these and you can be very proud of yourself. It's really important that you know about the book's historical context — so make sure you can answer all these questions without any problems before you turn over to the next section.

In-depth Questions

1) How does the historical background of the American South help to explain why the black community in Maycomb is treated badly?

2) Briefly explain who the Ku Klux Klan were and what they believed in.

3) Pick a scene that shows the reality of what life was like in 1930s America. How do you think it shows this?

4) Find an example from the novel that shows a character who is proud to be from the South.

5) Why wasn't the New Deal more effective in improving the Southern economy?

6) What do you think is a possible reason for Mr Cunningham's racism?

7) How is the Civil Rights Movement relevant to *To Kill a Mockingbird*?

Analysis of Chapters 1 and 2 — Scout Starts School

This next section isn't going to make much sense unless you know the book upside down and inside out. If it's a summary of the plot you're after, flick to pages 6-7. But if it's top-mark analysis you want, look no further.

The story is narrated by Scout

© Karl Andre Photography Limited

1) The story is told from the perspective of an older Scout Finch looking back on the events of her childhood through the eyes of her younger self.
2) This first-person narrative allows *To Kill a Mockingbird* to explore two of its central themes — innocence and growing up.
3) As well as Scout, these chapters also introduce some of the other important characters — the other Finches, the Ewells, the Cunninghams and Boo Radley.

Maycomb has a lot of history

1) The opening chapters cover a lot of the history of the Finch family and Maycomb.
2) Generations of the Finch family made a living farming cotton on the family homestead, Finch's Landing. But Atticus doesn't do what people expect him to — instead of farming cotton he works as a lawyer. This hints that he's not afraid to do things differently.
3) Maycomb has been affected by the Great Depression. Scout says there was "nothing to buy and no money to buy it with" — this suggests that families and businesses are struggling to get by financially.

For more on the Great Depression look at p.10.

There's already a lot of prejudice in Maycomb

1) Maycomb gossips about the Radley family because they're different — they don't leave their house or involve themselves in Maycomb society.
2) Even Scout, Jem and Dill are prejudiced against Boo Radley — they turn him into a monster with "rotten" teeth, "blood-stained" hands and eyes that "popped".
3) The children are also suspicious of Miss Caroline because she's from Winston County — a part of Alabama that joined the Northern States in the Civil War (see p.8). This shows how grudges and prejudices are being passed down to the children.
4) The behaviour of families in Maycomb is predictable — all the Ewells are "trash" and all the Cunninghams don't take anything "they can't pay back". There's nothing to suggest that things are going to change.

Themes — Racism and Innocence

The children's portrayal of Boo Radley as a monster is an innocent childhood game. However, like the adults' racial prejudices, it could also be based on gossip, misunderstanding and fear.

"Don't blame me when he gouges your eyes out."

It's clear that the children are genuinely scared of Boo. It takes all of Jem's courage just to touch the Radley house. At this point there certainly seems to be something creepy and mysterious about the Radleys...

Analysis of Chapters 3 to 5 — Gifts in the Tree

One of the book's themes is education, and in these chapters Scout learns a lot of valuable life lessons from Atticus and Miss Maudie.

Scout learns to see things from other people's point of view

After her disastrous first day at school, Atticus encourages Scout to see things from Miss Caroline's point of view — he encourages her to "climb into [her] skin and walk around in it". He's trying to teach her to empathise with other people.

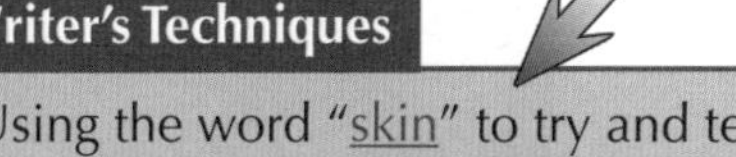

Using the word "skin" to try and teach Scout about tolerance hints at one of the novel's main themes — prejudice against people of a different race.

© Moviestore Collection Ltd

Scout learns from Miss Maudie

1) Scout learns a lot about life from Miss Maudie — she's a level-headed mother figure and a good role model to Scout.
2) Miss Maudie tells Scout that "one sprig of nut-grass can ruin a whole yard" — this is a metaphor for the damage that prejudice can cause in society.
3) Although Miss Maudie doesn't go about "doing good" like Miss Crawford, Scout has "faith" in her — this shows that she already understands the difference between appearances and reality.

Boo Radley becomes more human

Throughout the book, how the children treat Boo reflects their maturity. At the start, they're afraid of him, but they slowly begin to sympathise with him and by the end of the book they have come to respect him.

1) Boo starts leaving presents for the children in the knothole of a tree — his actions are kind and friendly.
2) Miss Maudie tells Scout that she knew Boo when he was younger and that he was a polite boy. She hints that his religious father keeps him locked up. This makes the reader — and Scout — feel sorry for him.
3) By showing the reader that the children's initial view of Boo was wrong, Harper Lee's showing us the importance of forming our own opinions, rather than just assuming that what Scout tells us is right.

Write about the life lessons Scout is learning...

Miss Maudie and Atticus try to teach Scout about life, whilst Jem scares her with ghost stories. Make sure you mention the way that Scout reacts to these things, and how they affect her character as she grows up.

Analysis of Chapters 6 to 8 — Snow and Fire

Things go a bit crazy in these chapters — there's snow in Maycomb and Miss Maudie's house burns down. These events may seem a bit random, but they tell us a lot about Maycomb society.

Jem starts to grow up

© Moviestore Collection Ltd

1) Jem is becoming more mature. He realises it was Boo who mended his trousers and he starts to doubt if he's a monster after all — Jem is starting to get rid of his prejudices about Boo.
2) The children find more gifts in the tree, until Nathan Radley fills the knothole with cement claiming that the tree is "dying".
3) The children's reactions to this show their different levels of maturity — Scout's sad because there won't be any more gifts, but Jem's upset because he understands that the knothole was a way for Boo to communicate with them and taking it away is cruel.

Maycomb has the coldest winter for a very long time

1) The characters' reactions to the snowfall in chapter 8 tell the reader a lot about what Maycomb is like:
   - School's cancelled even though there's hardly any snow — this suggests that Maycomb overreacts to unfamiliarity.
   - Eula May phones all the homes to tell the children school's cancelled — this shows how small the community is.
   - Mr Avery thinks the snow is a result of the children misbehaving — there's still a lot of superstition in the town.
2) Because there's only a bit of snow the children use a mound of dirt covered in snow to make a snowman. The outside of the snowman is white, but beneath the snow he's black. This symbolises how everybody is the same on the inside, regardless of skin colour.

The fire brings out the best in people

1) Miss Maudie's house burns down in the middle of the night but people are on hand to help her.
2) Mr Avery almost gets stuck trying to get her furniture out of the house and Miss Crawford lets Miss Maudie stay with her. This shows how the community is essentially good and the disaster has brought out the best in people.
3) Scout doesn't notice when Boo Radley puts a blanket round her shoulders. When she finds out it was him, she's not grateful and it makes her feel a bit sick — she still has prejudices about him.

Writer's Techniques

Snow and fire are pretty uncommon in Maycomb — they foreshadow the destructive events later in the book.

"It's bad children like you makes the seasons change."

Mr Avery thinks that the snow's a punishment for the bad behaviour of the children. He's a fine one to talk about bad behaviour — he urinates off his own porch. Brings a whole new meaning to peeing it down...

Analysis of Chapters 9 to 11 — The Mad Dog

The events in these chapters — Scout standing up to Cecil, Atticus shooting the dog and Mrs Dubose kicking her morphine habit — are all about courage. They help to build up to the biggie — Tom Robinson's courage.

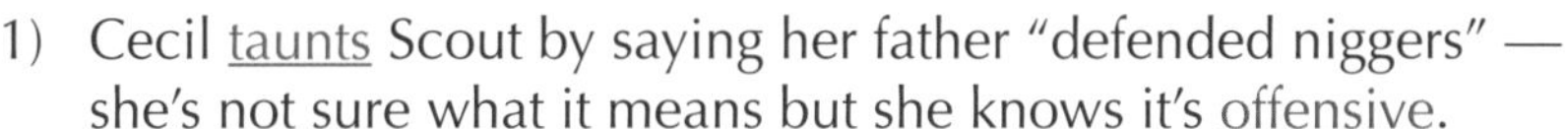

Scout has her first brush with racial prejudice

1) Cecil taunts Scout by saying her father "defended niggers" — she's not sure what it means but she knows it's offensive.
2) Scout walks away from a fight with Cecil — this is significant because she's beginning to learn that violence doesn't solve anything. Her restraint doesn't last long though — later in the chapter she beats up Francis for insulting Atticus.
3) Atticus tells the children he's going to defend Tom Robinson. He knows he's going to lose the trial, but he accepts the case anyway — he wouldn't respect himself if he didn't fight for justice.

Atticus is a deadly shot

1) Jem and Scout think their father is "feeble" because he doesn't shoot, smoke or play football.
2) When Atticus shoots the rabid dog the children finally respect him, but Atticus doesn't want the children to look up to him for something so deadly.
3) The rabid dog is a symbol for prejudice. Atticus protects Maycomb from a "mad dog" just like he tries to protect the town from the madness of prejudice later in the book.

© Moviestore Collection Ltd

Theme — Racism

Scout thinks mad dogs "foamed at the mouth" and "lunged at throats" — the reality is much more subtle. This is similar to how white people think that black people are a danger to the community but the real threat — white people's prejudice — is harder to spot.

Jem chops down Mrs Dubose's flowers

1) Although she's a grumpy, racist old woman, Atticus admires Mrs Dubose because she wants to die free of her morphine addiction.
2) Atticus says that it doesn't matter if she dies free or not — she's brave to have tried. Tom Robinson's trial is the same — Atticus knows that he can't win, but trying shows true courage.

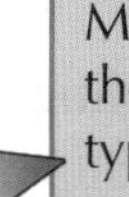

Theme — Bravery

Mrs Dubose's actions teach the children about different types of bravery and that courage isn't just a "man with a gun in his hand".

3) Mrs Dubose gives Jem a box with a camellia flower inside — he thinks she's taunting him. But the flower actually represents her goodness — it's a sign of forgiveness and thanks. When Jem keeps the flower but throws the box on the fire it suggests that he still has mixed feelings about Mrs Dubose but he's beginning to understand about people's complexity.

Lee presents courage in different forms...

As Jem begins to understand, different characters are brave in different ways — it's one of the ways that Harper Lee shows that her characters are complex. There's more about the theme of bravery on p.52.

Analysis of Chapters 12 to 14 — Dill Runs Away

Welcome to Part Two — these chapters deal a lot with the idea of identity. Cal leads a double life, Aunt Alexandra is obsessed with family status and Dill feels like he doesn't belong.

The children visit the black community's church

1) The black community worship in the church on Sundays but on weekdays "white men gambled in it" — this shows that the white people don't have much respect for the black community
2) Lee represents the black community positively — most of the congregation welcome Jem and Scout and they raise money to help the Robinsons. This is important because it makes the white people's racism seem even more irrational.
3) However, the black people have faults too — Lula is prejudiced against Scout and Jem and some of the members of the congregation are reluctant to part with their money.
4) Calpurnia speaks differently when she's with other black people. This shows how big the divide is between the communities — there's a division not only of class but language too.

Writer's Techniques

By making all the characters in the novel (both black and white) have faults, Lee makes them seem more like real people.

Aunt Alexandra turns up

1) Aunt Alexandra represents another kind of prejudice — social snobbery. She thinks family identity is important — she wants Scout and Jem to live up to the family name.
2) Aunt Alexandra thinks that "the longer a family had been squatting on one patch of land the finer it was", but Scout thinks that "fine folks" are people who "did the best they could with the sense they had".

Theme — Innocence

Scout's a lot more perceptive than Aunt Alexandra about what it means to be "fine folks". In this case her innocence makes her more moral.

Dill hides under the bed

1) Dill runs away from home and Scout and Jem find him under Scout's bed. Jem breaks the "remaining code of... childhood" by telling Atticus — this shows Jem's maturity and the widening gap between him and Scout.
2) Dill explains he ran away because his parents weren't "interested" in him. It's significant that Dill runs away to the Finches' — it's a place where he feels loved and wanted.

"I never understood her preoccupation with heredity."

Aunt Alexandra's a bit of a snob — she doesn't think any family in Maycomb is as good as the Finches. Jem finds this funny, considering just about every family in Maycomb is related to them in some way.

Analysis of Chapters 15 to 17 — The Trial Begins

Things start to get a bit nasty and the Maycomb residents start to show their true colours. Some people think Atticus shouldn't be defending a black man, and they aren't afraid to speak their minds...

Atticus is threatened by a lynch mob

1) Atticus sits outside the jail because he knows a lynch mob is coming to get Tom — he wants to protect him.
2) The mob are a bunch of drunkards and cowards — they smell of "whisky" and threaten 12-year-old Jem. Lee portraying them in this way makes them seem pathetic.
3) Scout spots Mr Cunningham in the mob and asks about his entailment and his son. This reminds Cunningham that he owes a lot to Atticus and that he's a father, just like Atticus.

There are some complex people in Maycomb

1) A lot of the characters in the novel aren't completely good or completely bad.
2) At the start of the book, Mr Cunningham is presented as an honest, hard-working man. The reader sees him differently when he joins the lynch mob.

Writer's Techniques

Harper Lee's characters have a mixture of good and bad qualities — just like real people do. This makes them more believable and shows the reader that it's important not to judge on first impressions.

3) Judge Taylor appears incompetent — he puts his feet up on the desk and sometimes looks as though he's falling asleep. But in reality he has a "firm grip" on the trial.
4) Bob Ewell is less complicated — he's a dirty drunkard who lives behind a dump. He's also a horrible person — he lies to destroy an innocent man.

Writer's Techniques

The way Lee describes Bob is an example of the bird symbolism in the book. He's described as a "bantam cock" — this suggests he's showing off. He's confident that he's going to win the trial and he's enjoying the attention from the community which usually ignores him. For more detail turn to p.59.

There's prejudice in the court before the trial even begins

1) The courthouse is segregated — the black people are separated from the white people. It's symbolic that Scout, Jem and Dill sit with the black people — they're seeing things from a black person's perspective both literally and metaphorically.
2) The jury is made up of farmers and people who look like "dressed-up Cunninghams". As Mr Cunningham was part of the lynch mob the reader knows that they'll be prejudiced before the trial even starts.

"I discovered that these men were strangers."

In another book, the scene outside the jail might have been preachy or too far-fetched, but the fact Scout doesn't really understand the danger she's in until the next day makes the whole thing more effective.

Analysis of Chapters 18 to 20 — Tom Testifies

There are lots of subtle things to pick up on in these chapters like the portrayal of characters, the deeper meaning of Miss Maudie's absence from court and what the language of the courtroom reveals.

Mayella is a victim too

1) Mayella is lonely and unhappy — she has to look after seven children and her father is abusive.
2) Tom recognises she has a tough life and says that he feels sorry for her — the court are shocked that he'd dare to pity a white person.

Theme — Racism

The court are shocked by the fact that Tom pities Mayella because he has even less social standing than she does.

Only the racist white people attend the trial

Photograph by Leigh Toldi

1) Scout and Dill bump into Dolphus Raymond outside the courtroom. They discover that he isn't really a drunk — the reason he pretends is so that Maycomb can use his drunkenness as an excuse for the fact that he's not like the other people in the town.
2) Link Deas tries to vouch for Tom's character — but this gets him thrown out of the court.
3) The fact that non-racist characters like Miss Maudie and Dolphus Raymond don't attend the trial is important. They know Tom will be found guilty and they don't want to see him sent to his death.

The language reveals a lot about respect

1) When Atticus talks politely to Mayella she thinks he's teasing her — she's not used to courtesy.
2) Tom speaks politely in court — he calls Atticus "Mr Finch" and "suh" whereas Bob Ewell's language is coarse and disrespectful. In Chapter 17, he says Tom was "ruttin'" on Mayella — the reader sympathises with Tom and dislikes Ewell even more.
3) Mr Gilmer calls Tom Robinson "Robinson" and "boy". Dill doesn't understand why Mr Gilmer is so "hateful" to Tom — it's because he doesn't respect Tom and he's prejudiced too.
4) The way Mr Gilmer speaks to Tom upsets Dill — this shows how strong an effect it has on him — usually things don't register with Dill because he's so childlike.

Theme — Racism

The fact that in Chapter 21 the jury end up siding with Bob Ewell even though he's so disrespectful shows just how prejudiced they are.

Mention that Tom and Atticus are sure to lose the case...

Writing about the inevitable outcome of the case will show that you understand the depth of racial prejudice in the novel. There's good evidence that Tom couldn't have done it, but that won't be enough...

Analysis of Chapters 21 to 23 — The Verdict

The jury reach a verdict and Tom's found guilty — the children can't believe it. They realise first-hand just how unfair prejudice can be.

The trial disillusions the children

1) Jem's convinced that the jury will find Tom innocent — but they return a guilty verdict. Jem's naivety shows that he still has a lot to learn about prejudice.
2) Dill's disillusioned by the trial — he wants to become a clown because there's not much he can do about people "except laugh".
3) Jem idealistic view of the world has been shattered. He thinks people "go out of their way to despise each other", and this makes him realise that Boo might not want to come outside. He's learnt to empathise with Boo.

Theme — Growing up

Even Dill, the most childlike of the group, is becoming cynical. But he wants to be a "new kind of clown" — he wants things to change.

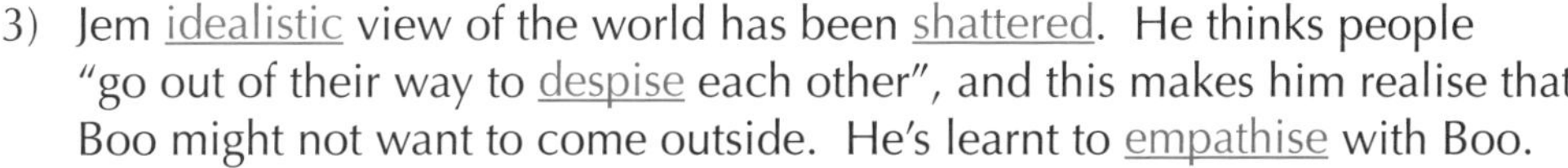

But there's hope for the future

1) The black community stand up when Atticus leaves the courtroom — they respect him and appreciate what he's tried to do.
2) Atticus tells Jem that a member of the jury wanted to acquit Tom, which was the reason the jury took so long to reach a verdict. The fact that someone on the jury thought he was innocent gives the reader hope that things might change in the future.
3) Judge Taylor chose Atticus to be Tom's lawyer because he thought he'd be the most likely to give Tom a good chance at justice.
4) Atticus warns that things will change. He says that one day white people will "pay the bill" for their treatment of black people.

© Everett Collection/Rex Features

Writer's Techniques

When the book was published America was finally beginning to change — black people had begun campaigning for equality. For more information have a look at p.11.

Aunt Alexandra is still harping on about family

1) It turns out that the member of the jury who wanted to acquit Tom was a Cunningham. This gives Scout a new respect for Walter Cunningham. But Aunt Alexandra doesn't want Scout hanging out with Walter because "he - is - trash". The trial hasn't taught Alexandra anything about her own social prejudices.
2) Jem is beginning to understand the social class system. He tells Scout that there are "four kinds of folks in the world". But Scout is still too innocent to accept this and says: "there's just one kind of folks. Folks."

"Judge Taylor's voice came from far away, and was tiny."

As the verdict arrives, Scout remembers her dad killing the rabid dog. Atticus seemed all-powerful then, but now even he can't protect her from knowing that their neighbours have just condemned an innocent man.

Analysis of Chapters 24 to 26 — Tom's Death

Scout begins to respect Aunt Alexandra a bit more in these chapters — she sympathises with Atticus, is horrified by Tom's death and keeps her composure in front of the missionary ladies.

Scout learns to be considerate

1) Scout's beginning to grow up and think about other people. She wears a dress and attends the missionary tea because she knows that it'll please Aunt Alexandra.
2) Scout's not afraid of the Radley place any more and she feels "remorse" for tormenting Boo — this shows her maturity. However, it's a sign of lost innocence too — Scout says that Boo is now "the least of our fears".

Theme — Growing up

Scout fantasises about meeting Boo and saying "'Hidy do, Mr Arthur'" — she doesn't see him as a monster any more.

Maycomb's women don't see their own hypocrisy

- The women of Maycomb are sympathetic to the "sin and squalor" of the Mruna tribe in Africa but they aren't willing to help out the poor black community on their own doorstep.
- Mrs Merriweather thinks the people in the North of America are hypocrites because although they wanted to abolish slavery they don't treat black people as equals. Because Southern states like Alabama didn't want to abolish slavery she thinks Maycomb doesn't have the "sin" of hypocrisy "on our shoulders".
- She also says there's "nothing more distracting than a sulky darky" and blames Atticus for stirring up the black community. She doesn't realise that her own prejudices have an effect too.
- Miss Gates tells the children that Hitler's persecution of Jews is wrong. Scout thinks this is hypocritical — she doesn't see how Maycomb's persecution of black people is any different. This shows how the characters are aware of prejudice but blind to their own.

There are mixed reactions to Tom's death

1) When Helen Robinson hears the news about Tom's death she falls to the ground as if "a big foot just came along and stepped on her". This is similar to the bit at the beginning of Chapter 25 where Jem stops Scout from squashing a bug — like an insect, Helen is weak and defenceless.
2) Maycomb is only interested in Tom's death for "perhaps two days" — this shows how unimportant it is to them.
3) They think that attempting to run is "typical" of a black man — he was obviously guilty if he tried to escape.
4) Mr Underwood compares Tom's death to the "senseless slaughter of songbirds". This reminds the reader of Chapter 10 when Atticus tells Scout and Jem that they must never kill a mockingbird, and it encourages the reader to think that Tom is the mockingbird the title refers to.

EXAM TIP

Look at how some characters are blind to their prejudices...

Show that you understand the hypocrisy of the women in Maycomb, e.g. Mrs Merriweather wants to help the Mruna tribe, but ignores the problems on her own doorstep. Not very Christian behaviour, Mrs M.

Analysis of Chapters 27 to 29 — The Attack

Chapter 27 is quite a funny chapter with the description of the trick the kids play on Miss Tutti and Miss Frutti, but there's a hint of what's to come in the other chapters with Aunt Alexandra's feeling of apprehension...

There's calm before the storm

1) Things "settle down" for a bit — the town goes back to the "familiar routine of school, play, study".
2) The Missionary ladies are still talking about the Mruna tribe, where a "child had as many fathers as there were men in the community". The women pity the Mrunas for this, which is ironic because the Mrunas' society seems more unified than Maycomb's.
3) A lull in the drama adds realism to the story, but it also builds the tension for the final chapters.

Foreshadowing builds the tension

1) Bob Ewell starts to threaten people connected with the trial. His actions are cowardly — he follows Helen because he knows she's defenceless and he only breaks into Judge Taylor's house because he thought the judge was out.
2) The setting of Chapter 28 is also significant. It's Halloween and it's "pitch black" — this creates a scary atmosphere.
3) Scout goes to a Halloween booth where she has to touch "human" body parts — it's a foreshadowing of her touching Bob Ewell's corpse in the next chapter.

Writer's Techniques

Foreshadowing is when the writer hints at something that will happen later on in the novel. For more on foreshadowing and the ways that Harper Lee creates tension, turn to p.55.

Photograph by Leigh Toldi

Bob Ewell attacks the children

KEY EVENT

1) Bob attacks Jem and Scout as they're walking home from the pageant — this shows his true cowardice because they're just defenceless children.
2) During the attack, Scout is blinded by her costume so she can't see what's happening. This builds suspense because the reader is just as confused as she is.
3) Ewell tries to stab Scout but she's protected by her costume — her childish innocence has saved her again, just like when the mob threatens Atticus outside the jail.

Writer's Techniques

When Bob Ewell attacks the children it's a shocking moment for the reader. The reader underestimates how evil Bob is, just like Atticus does. This is because the idea that a grown man would attempt to get revenge by stabbing vulnerable children is disturbing and unexpected.

"He was running, running towards us with no child's steps."

Scout's confusion adds to the tension of the attack, but the reader can still figure out some details that she can't. For example, we know that Jem's not dead, because of the information at the very start of the book.

Analysis of Chapters 30 and 31 — Boo is Revealed

So here are the final chapters. Pat yourself on the back for making it to the end (unless you've just skipped to the last page, in which case shame on you). This is where Harper Lee ties everything up in a nice neat bow..

Boo is revealed

KEY EVENT

1) After 29 chapters of anticipation the reader finally meets Boo.
2) He has "the voice of a child", and is pale with "feathery" hair — this makes the reader think of the feathers on a mockingbird.
3) As well as being revealed physically, Boo's character is also revealed — he's not a monster at all, he's a brave but shy man.

Justice is finally served

1) Heck Tate tries to investigate Bob's death — Atticus thinks Jem killed Bob in self-defence but Heck Tate thinks Jem couldn't have stabbed Bob with his broken arm.
2) Heck claims Bob fell on his knife and killed himself. However Harper Lee hints that Heck thinks Boo was the one who killed Bob — Heck says: "I never heard tell that it's against the law for a citizen to do his utmost to prevent a crime from being committed, which is exactly what he did".
3) He convinces Atticus to agree that Bob killed himself — "Let the dead bury the dead this time, Mr Finch."
4) Heck thinks it would be a sin to drag Boo "with his shy ways into the limelight". He's trying to protect Boo from being accused of Ewell's death — he doesn't want Boo to go to court and suffer at the hands of local prejudice like Tom Robinson did.

Writer's Techniques

This echoes the court proceedings — it's the second time that a damaged arm has been used to prove someone's innocence.

Scout's come a long way... but she's still a child

1) The novel is a bildungsroman — a novel where growing up is one of the central themes. It's typical of this kind of novel that the main character reflects on what they've learnt.
2) Scout has learnt to be sensitive — she walks Boo home but makes it look like he's the one escorting her — she wants to protect him from gossip.
3) She's also finally learnt the importance of empathy — she says, "you never really know a man until you stand in his shoes and walk around in them."
4) Although she's learnt a lot she's still naive in some ways. She says "there wasn't much else left for us to learn, except possibly algebra", and falls asleep on Atticus's lap — the reader knows she's still innocent. This peaceful ending gives the reader hope that society will be more equal when Scout grows up.

KEY QUOTE

"his voice was so deep and his knee was so snug that I slept."

Some authors might have ended the book with Scout's dawning understanding on the Radley porch. But I like it better this way — everyone at home, safe and sound, and Atticus watching over his son. Awww.

Practice Questions

So that, in a nutshell, was 'To Kill a Mockingbird'. Hopefully you've read the book all the way through at least once as well. Have a go at these questions to see how much you know already. You should be able to answer the Quick Questions with just a few words or a sentence. Good luck to you.

Quick Questions — Chapters 1-14

1) Who is the novel narrated by?
2) Why are the children suspicious of Miss Caroline?
3) Where does Boo put his gifts for the children?
4) What does Mr Avery think caused the freak snowfall?
5) Who puts a blanket round Scout's shoulders the night Miss Maudie's house burns down?
6) Why does Scout get into a fight with Francis?
7) Who shoots and kills the dog in chapter 10?
8) Who was trying to beat their morphine addiction before they died?
9) Who makes the children feel unwelcome at the black church?
10) Who runs away and hides under Scout's bed?

Practice Questions

And now for the Quick Questions on the second half of the novel...

Quick Questions — Chapters 15-31

11) Why does Atticus sit outside the county jail?

12) Who does Harper Lee describe as a "bantam cock" in chapter 17?

13) Give two reasons why the reader might feel sorry for Mayella.

14) Why does Mayella think Atticus is teasing her?

15) Name two characters who don't attend Tom Robinson's trial.

16) Why does Scout want to play with Walter Cunningham?

17) What reason does Jem give for Boo staying indoors in chapter 23?

18) What protects Scout from Bob Ewell's knife when he tries to stab her?

19) Who comes to the children's rescue when Bob Ewell attacks them?

20) How do we know that Scout hasn't lost all of her innocence by the end of the book?

Character Profile — Scout Finch

Scout is the narrator of *To Kill a Mockingbird* — the whole story is told from her point of view. Because she's just a child she doesn't always understand what's happening around her.

Scout isn't a typical young girl

1) Scout's a tomboy — she spends most of her time playing with boys, she hates wearing dresses and she isn't afraid to get into fights.
2) Scout doesn't just accept things — she's inquisitive and questions how people behave. For example, she doesn't understand why Aunt Alexandra tells her not to say certain things in front of Calpurnia.
3) She's got a bit of a temper — she punches Francis for calling Atticus a "nigger-lover" — but her flaws make her a well-rounded, believable character.

Writer's Techniques

Making Scout inquisitive encourages the reader to question their own behaviour and the behaviour of others.

Photograph by Leigh Toldi

Scout is...

fearless: "I split my knuckle to the bone on his front teeth"

inquisitive: "'do you think Boo Radley's still alive?'"

innocent: "there wasn't much else left for us to learn, except possibly algebra"

Scout's character develops over the course of the book

Scout's character changes as she gets older. Here are a few examples:

In the opening chapters Scout torments and gossips about Boo.

In the final chapter, Scout learns to see things from Boo's point of view.

In Chapter 3 Scout thinks it's OK to be rude to Walter because "he's just a Cunningham".

At the end of the novel Scout respects Walter's family because one of them thought Tom Robinson was innocent.

Scout uses words like "nigger" without thought — she doesn't think it's offensive to use those kinds of words.

The older Scout uses the more respectful word "Negro" instead — for more on the importance of language look at p.57.

She's childlike — she wants to play with her big brother and gets cross when he doesn't want to play with her.

She addresses some adult issues — she asks Atticus what rape is and she's curious about how the legal system works.

Although Scout is still a child at the end of the book and keeps a lot of her innocence, the events of the book have forced her to grow up fast. She's more perceptive and empathic at the end of the book because of what she's learnt.

Comment on the ways in which Scout changes...

As Scout grows up, she starts to question the prejudice she sees. Harper Lee makes her such a likeable, well-rounded character that it's easy for the reader to agree with her and empathise with her point of view.

Character Profile — Atticus Finch

Atticus is Scout and Jem's dad, and he's really the central character in *To Kill a Mockingbird*. He's a popular man from a respected Maycomb family and his court case is vital to the book's plot.

Atticus is a lawyer who works hard to do a good job

Atticus is a lawyer but he doesn't just do the job for financial reasons — he cares about his clients and accepts things like hickory nuts as payment from poorer people.

Atticus is...

respectful: "I do my best to love everybody"
patient: "infinite capacity for calming turbulent seas"
fair: "We trust him to do right."

He's honourable and unselfish

1) Atticus does his best to defend Tom Robinson even though he knows that a lot of people in Maycomb won't like him for it. He says there's been talk in the town that he "shouldn't do much about defending this man".

2) Defending Tom Robinson shows how important Atticus's job is to his sense of self-worth — he says that if he didn't try his best he wouldn't be able to "hold up my head in town".

Theme — Racism

Because of the discriminatory way black people were treated at that time, Atticus knows that he has little chance of winning the case for Tom Robinson. But he's a man of high principles and he does what's right even when other people disagree with him.

Atticus is a good father

- He teaches Scout and Jem to accept people's social and racial differences and not to judge people because of them.
- He is always honest with his children, and tries to answer their questions truthfully.
- He spends time with his children — reading, kicking a ball around and talking to them — this would've been unusual for fathers of that time.

Theme — Family and Social Class

Atticus contrasts with the other fathers in the book — Dill's father isn't interested in him, Bob Ewell mistreats his children and Mr Radley tries to keep Boo indoors.

Character Profile — Atticus Finch

Atticus earns everyone's respect by respecting everyone

1) Atticus is courteous to everybody, regardless of their race, social class or behaviour towards him. He sees the good in everybody and tries to encourage his children to do the same.
2) For example, even though Mrs Dubose says offensive things about Atticus he's still courteous to her — he's polite to everyone. For more about Atticus's language flick to p.57.
3) Atticus isn't hypocritical and doesn't have double standards, unlike most of the people of Maycomb. He's "the same in his house as he is on the public streets".
4) He practises what he preaches. He teaches his children to be honest, empathic and fair — just like he is.
5) He provides a voice for the black community when he takes on Tom Robinson's case. But he also recognises when he needs a black person to communicate for him — for example when he takes Calpurnia with him to tell Helen that Tom's dead.

He's still human though

1) Sometimes he gets angry or loses his temper, like when he "fusses" or has a "fierce discussion" with Aunt Alexandra.
2) He's disheartened when he loses the trial — "If I don't wake up in the morning, don't call me."
3) He misjudges Bob Ewell's threats: "What on earth could Ewell do to me, sister?" His faith in people almost gets his children killed.

Writer's Techniques

Harper Lee balances out Atticus's character to make him more realistic so the reader empathises with him more.

He's different from the rest of Maycomb's men

1) At the start of the book Jem and Scout don't appreciate their father — they think he's "feeble" because "he was nearly fifty."
2) But Atticus isn't afraid to be different from the rest of Maycomb's men — he's academic, he doesn't drink and spends his evenings reading with his family. In Maycomb, people are judged for being different, but because the town respects Atticus they accept the way he is.

For more on Maycomb's men turn to p.39.

Compare Atticus with other fathers in the novel...

Atticus has a few minor flaws, but there's no denying he's a good father, unlike lots of the other fathers in the novel. In the exam you could compare him to Mr Radley, Mr Ewell or Dill's absent father.

Character Profile — Jem Finch

Jem is Scout's big brother. He's four years older than she is but they're really close and they do a lot of thing together. The first and last lines of the novel are about Jem. This reflects how important he is to the story.

Jem grows up the most

1) All the children grow up over the course of the book — but it's Jem who develops the most.

Jem is...

brave: "In all his life, Jem had never declined a dare."

sensitive: "How could they do it, how could they?"

calm: "he had a naturally tranquil disposition"

2) Scout starts to notice Jem's new maturity in Chapter 6. She says: "It was then, I suppose, that Jem and I first began to part company."
3) Jem "broke the remaining code of our childhood" by telling Atticus about Dill running away from home — he's trying to be responsible.
4) He explains things to Scout like the court case — he understands things better than she does.
5) After the trial Jem stops Scout killing an insect — Tom Robinson's case has taught him how important it is to protect the weak.
6) He looks after Scout. When she messes up the school pageant Jem's sympathetic. He makes Scout "feel right when things went wrong".

He can sometimes be a bit of a rebel

Jem's more level-headed than Scout, but he isn't always respectful and won't always do what he's told:

- He sometimes lies to avoid getting into trouble — for example, he lies to Atticus when he loses his trousers running away from the Radley house.
- He torments Boo, even though Atticus has told him to leave him alone.
- He destroys Mrs Dubose's camellias.
- He refuses to go home and leave Atticus with the mob outside the jail.

Jem shows his feelings quite a lot

1) Jem's sensitive — he worries about Atticus when he sits outside the jail. This also shows how the roles are beginning to reverse — Jem wants to look after his father.
2) He's clearly upset by the outcome of the trial — his hands go white from gripping the balcony rail when he hears the jury say "guilty", and his shoulders jerk as if each verdict "was a separate stab between them". The verdict also makes him cry.
3) He has a strong sense of justice. He knows that what happens to Tom Robinson isn't right.

© Karl Andre Photography Limited

"Scout, I think I'm beginning to understand something."

Jem grows up through the story but Scout finds the changes in him frustrating at times, as if he's leaving her behind. It's clear that he understands what's going on in the community much better than she does.

Character Profile — Aunt Alexandra and Uncle Jack

Aunt Alexandra is Atticus's sister. Uncle Jack is his younger brother. They all grew up together at Finch's Landing — the old family home.

Aunt Alexandra is a proud lady

1) Unlike Atticus and Uncle Jack, Aunt Alexandra hasn't moved away from Finch's Landing — this suggests she's not as open-minded as her brothers. She's the most conservative and prejudiced of the Finches.
2) She's proud of her family and background. She tries hard to make Scout and Jem understand their family connections and to have pride in their family — with little success.
3) She fits into Maycomb society "like a hand into a glove" — she's the perfect hostess and has "boarding-school manners".
4) Later in the book Lee develops her character and we see her more caring and sensitive side. She's horrified by Tom's death and it's clear she's been worried about Atticus.

She has some prejudices of her own

1) Aunt Alexandra can be racist — she thinks it's wrong for Scout and Jem to go to Cal's church, and doesn't think that a black servant should have so much to do with their upbringing.

Aunt Alexandra is...

interfering: "Aunty had a way of declaring What Is Best For The Family"

a busybody: "she was an incurable gossip"

dignified: "if Aunty could be a lady at a time like this, so could I"

2) Her grandson Francis repeats some of the racist things he's heard her say — he's been brought up to think black people are inferior.
3) She's also a snob and has social prejudices too — she doesn't think any family in Maycomb is as good as the Finches.
4) Harper Lee includes Aunt Alexandra to provide a different point of view from the rest of the Finches. But because her character begins to sympathise with the Robinson family by the end of the book she also gives the reader hope that traditional Southern views can change.

Uncle Jack keeps his word

1) Uncle Jack is ten years younger than Atticus. Atticus paid for him to study medicine.
2) He respects the children and honours his promise to Scout to not tell Atticus about the real reason for her fight with Francis.
3) But Scout tells him, "you don't understand children much" and Jack realises she's right. He didn't let Scout tell her side of the story after the fight and he isn't as honest with the children as Atticus is.

Mention that Aunt Alexandra has a sensitive side too...

Aunt Alexandra starts out a right old boot, but after Chapter 24 I quite like her. Like nearly every character in the novel, she has good and bad points — make sure you talk about why Lee creates characters like this.

Character Profile — Dill

Dill is Scout and Jem's friend who comes to Maycomb every summer. The character of Dill is probably base on Harper Lee's childhood friend, Truman Capote, who went on to become a famous writer just like her.

Dill is a little boy with a big imagination

1) Dill comes to Maycomb every summer and stays with his Aunt Rach He's from Mississippi and his full name is Charles Baker Harris.
2) He plays with Scout and Jem and comes up with all kinds of "eccentric plans".
3) He can be very honest. He tells the Finch family that his Aunt Rachel "drinks a pint for breakfast every morning". When Aunt Alexandra challenges this, he says he's just "Tellin' the truth".
4) He has an active imagination and often prefers to make things up rather than tell the truth. The reader gets the impression that he uses his imagination to escape from his unhappy home life.
5) He can be very innocent and childlike — he wants to marry Scout and "get" a baby

Theme — Innocence

Dill's innocent desire to have a baby shows how much he wants to be part of a secure, loving family.

He runs away from things that make him unhappy

1) Dill doesn't feel loved by his parents. He runs away from home because his family "just wasn't interested in me".
2) He's so upset at the way Tom Robinson is treated in the courtroom that he has to leave — he's running away from reality again.

Theme — Family Identity

Dill's miserable home life contrasts with the Finches' — Atticus provides his children with a loving, secure environment, which is why Dill goes there.

3) Dill says that he's going to be a clown when he's older as there's nothing you can do about people but laugh at them. It's another example of his escapism — he doesn't think things will change so he imagines running away to the circus to escape Maycomb's prejudice. For more on this, have a look at p.21.

Dill is...

imaginative: "Beautiful things floated around in his dreamy head."

childlike: "Dill had started crying and couldn't stop"

sensitive: "striking a match under a turtle was hateful"

"[his] head teemed with eccentric plans, strange longings"

Dill is a dreamy boy. He's not always truthful, but mainly because he prefers his stories to real life. He runs away to Maycomb because he's always passed around his family and he needs to feel wanted — bless him.

Character Profile — Calpurnia

Calpurnia used to work at Finch's Landing and is now Atticus's cook.
She's far more than just an employee — she's an important part of the Finch family.

Calpurnia teaches and disciplines the Finch children

1) Jem and Scout's mother died when they were young so Calpurnia helps Atticus raise his children.
2) She educates Scout — she teaches her to write by setting her writing tasks on rainy days.
3) She also teaches the children manners — she's furious with Scout when she criticises Walter Cunningham's table manners.
4) She isn't afraid to tell the children off — when she finds them in the courthouse she tells them they should be "'shamed of" themselves for being at the trial.
5) Atticus trusts Cal completely. When Scout complains that Cal is too strict Atticus responds, "you mind her, you hear?"

Photograph by Leigh Toldi

She really cares about the Finch family

1) She can be affectionate towards Scout. For example, she kisses her and makes her crackling bread after her first day at school, and calls her "baby" and "honey".
2) She's compassionate — she tells Scout to come and find her in the kitchen if she ever feels "lonesome", and Scout turns to Calpurnia as Jem grows more distant.

Calpurnia is...

strict: "She was always ordering me out of the kitchen"

valued: "We couldn't operate a single day without Cal"

stern: "I seldom pleased her and she seldom rewarded me."

Calpurnia is a link between the black and white communities

- Calpurnia changes how she speaks depending on who she's with. She talks "white folks' talk" with the Finches and "coloured folks' talk" when she's with black people. She has a strong sense of the two communities and understands the importance of fitting in. There's more on Cal's language on p.56-57.
- She teaches the children about the black community when she takes them to her church.
- She goes with Atticus to tell Helen Robinson that her husband's been shot — she provides support for them both.
- Calpurnia is one of the few black characters who can read and write — this is powerful as it gives hope that characters like her can use their education to change white people's attitudes and liberate the black community. For more on the power of education have a look at p.50 and p.57.

"We couldn't operate a single day without Cal"

Calpurnia is someone you can rely on. She's the one who warns everyone about the rabid dog — even the Radleys. And she stands up for Jem and Scout when Lula makes them feel unwelcome at the black church.

Character Profile — The Radley Family

The Radley family are the source of gossip in Maycomb because of their reclusive nature. Scout and Jem are curious about the Radleys' house, but also terrified by it.

The Radley family have always had a strange reputation

1) The Radley family never go to church and worship at home instead — this makes them different from everyone else in Maycomb.
2) They keep themselves to themselves — their doors are always shut and no one ever visits them.
3) Everyone seems to have an opinion about the elder Mr Radley. Miss Stephanie Crawford describes him as an "upright" and God-fearing man, but Calpurnia says he's "the meanest man ever God blew breath into".
4) The Radleys' house is seen as frightening and mysterious. People avoid walking past it at night and fruit from the garden is believed by the schoolchildren to be poisonous.

The Radleys are...

reclusive: "The shutters and doors of the Radley house were closed on Sundays"

dangerous: "Mr Radley shot a Negro in his collard patch."

mysterious: "people said the house died"

The story hints that Boo is mistreated

Remember there are two Mr Radleys — the older Mr Radley is Boo's father and the younge Mr Radley is Nathan, Boo's elder brother.

1) There are stories that Mr Radley's son Boo got in with the wrong crowd when he was younger. Mr Radley was ashamed of his son's behaviour and punished him by locking him up.
2) Jem wonders if Mr Radley restrains Boo to keep him in the house, but Atticus says there are "other ways of making people into ghosts" — hinting that Boo has been mistreated by his family.

Themes — Family Identity

Mr Radley is ashamed of his son's actions because they reflect on him. Mr Radley keeps Boo indoors so he can't embarrass him again — it's another example of how outward appearances and family reputation are the most important things to some people in Maycomb.

3) When Scout asks Miss Maudie about Mr Radley she says: "the Bible in the hand of one man is worse than a whisky bottle" in the hand of another. This suggests that Mr Radley's religious nature had a damaging effect on his family.
4) Mr Radley dies and his elder son, Nathan, arrives to take over the family house. But even after his father's death Boo still doesn't come out — this suggests that Nathan isn't much different from his father.
5) Boo leaves gifts for the children in the knothole of a tree — when Nathan finds out he fills the knothole with cement. He wants to stop Boo from communicating with the children — he's cruel.

Character Profile — The Radley Family

There are lots of stories about Boo

1) In the opening chapter Scout describes Boo as a "malevolent phantom" — he's portrayed as some kind of ghost or monster.
2) The community gossips about him — he's used as a scapegoat. People blame him when bad things happen in the neighbourhood.

A scapegoat is someone who gets blamed and punished for something that isn't their fault.

Boo is...

mysterious: "Mr Radley's boy was not seen again for fifteen years"

polite: "He always spoke nicely to me"

timid: "the voice of a child afraid of the dark"

Writer's Techniques

Harper Lee uses the children's descriptions of Boo to make the reader think that he's scary and horrible. But she slowly reveals what a kind and thoughtful man he is — she teaches the reader to not be influenced by other people's prejudices.

Boo is another innocent victim of the town's prejudice

1) Arthur Radley gradually shows himself to be a good, kind man — he's just been misunderstood.
2) He's lonely — he tries to make friends with Scout and Jem and leaves them presents in the tree — it's his way of trying to reach out to them.
3) He tries to help Jem and Scout whenever he can. He puts a blanket around Scout to keep her warm as she stands watching the fire, and he tries to sew Jem's trousers back together.
4) Boo must be keeping an eye on Scout and Jem — he's quickly at the scene when Bob Ewell attacks them. He wants to protect the children.
5) As Scout and Jem grow up, they learn to empathise with him. They realise that he's not an evil ghost but a shy man who needs his privacy. Jem realises that the reason Boo Radley has "stayed shut up in the house all this time..." is "because he *wants* to stay inside."

Writer's Techniques

Boo could be seen as the book's "mockingbird" — he's an innocent man and the things that he does for the children show that he's kind, but he's a victim of the town's prejudice nonetheless. For more on the symbolism of mockingbirds turn to p.59.

Write about how Lee creates secrecy around the Radleys...

Lee uses the children of Maycomb to make the Radley place seem spooky and mysterious — the children treat it like it's haunted, and although we know they're just kids, we can't help but be taken in by it all...

Character Profile — The Ewell Family

The Ewells are pretty famous in Maycomb — but for all the wrong reasons. They're like the nutty ones in a box of chocolates — no one really likes them.

The Ewells are rude and racist

1) The Ewell family are extremely poor. They live by a dump and make their shoes out of tyres.
2) But it's hard to feel sorry for them because they're not very nice people. Atticus describes them as the "disgrace of Maycomb".
3) Burris Ewell is in Scout's class at school:

- Like all his brothers and sisters Burris only comes to school on the first day. All the Ewell children are uneducated.
- Burris is dirty — he has "cooties" (head lice) and is the "filthiest human" Scout has ever seen.
- He's very rude to their teacher, calling her a "snot-nosed slut" and making her cry. Little Chuck Little, another child in the class, describes him as "a hard-down mean one".

Mayella Ewell has a hard life

1) Mayella Ewell is the oldest of the Ewell children and has to try and take care of the younger children because their mother's dead. She hasn't got any friends and doesn't even really know what friends are.
2) She thinks that Atticus is making fun of her when he calls her "ma'am" during the trial — she doesn't understand basic manners.
3) She's rude to Atticus in court and refuses to speak to him at all.
4) She's prejudiced — she refers to Tom Robinson as "nigger" and clearly thinks she has the right to make him do odd jobs for her.
5) Even though the reader is more likely to feel sorry for Mayella than the other Ewells it doesn't make her part in Tom's death any more forgivable.

Writer's Techniques

Although she lives surrounded by rubbish, Mayella grows red geraniums — this suggests that she's different from the rest of the Ewells because she hopes for a better life.

Mayella is...

dutiful: "accustomed to strenuous labour"

lonely: "Mayella Ewell must have been the loneliest person in the world"

neglected: "Tom Robinson was probably the only person who was ever decent to her."

Character Profile — The Ewell Family

Like Atticus, Bob Ewell is a widower and single parent trying to raise a young family alone — but that's where the similarities end. Even Atticus the eternal optimist couldn't find anything nice to say about him.

Bob Ewell is a particularly nasty character

1) Bob Ewell doesn't take care of his family and they live "like animals" — he's neglectful.
2) He's a bully — it's strongly hinted that he abuses his children.
3) Atticus believes that the whole idea of the accusation against Tom Robinson came from Bob Ewell as a cover story for beating Mayella: "'Who beat you up? Tom Robinson or your father?'" Because Bob made Mayella cry rape he's ultimately responsible for Tom Robinson's death.

Writer's Techniques

Bob Ewell is the only character in *To Kill a Mockingbird* who doesn't have any redeeming qualities. This ensures that the reader won't sympathise with him and makes the trial verdict even more shocking.

Bob Ewell is vindictive

1) During the trial he's arrogant and brash — he's confident he's going to win.
2) He's also relishing the fact that the townspeople are paying him attention — usually Maycomb treats him like "trash", but during the trial they're on his side.
3) But even though he wins the trial, Atticus and Judge Taylor make him look "like a fool". Bob realises this and vows to get revenge — he's ruthless and malicious.
4) Although he spits in Atticus's face and threatens him, Atticus doesn't think he's particularly dangerous. The fact that Atticus misjudges Bob is significant — he tries to see the good in Bob, but he's beyond any hope or forgiveness.
5) He attacks the defenceless characters. He terrorises Helen Robinson and tries to kill Jem and Scout — he's evil.

Bob's death at the end of the novel can be interpreted in a couple of ways. It might be that Bob Ewell was beyond hope and was killed by his own hate or that with his death justice has finally been done.

Bob is...

lazy: he was "fired from the WPA for laziness"

abusive: "She says what her papa do to her don't count."

arrogant: "his chest swelled, and once more he was a little red rooster"

"the disgrace of Maycomb for three generations."

I suppose the Ewell children were never really given a chance to turn out well, living next to a dump and never going to school — but that's no excuse for trying to get an innocent man convicted and executed.

Character Profile — The Robinson Family

Unlike the Ewells, the Robinsons are clean-living and respectable. Although Tom's arm was badly damaged in an accident, he still works hard to provide for his family.

Tom Robinson is a hard-working family man

Tom is 25 and lives with his wife Helen and their three children in a little settlement on the edge of town, not far from the Ewells. There's lots of evidence in the novel that Tom is a good man:

- He's a "faithful member" of his church.
- Calpurnia knows the Robinson family well. She says they're "clean-living folks".
- Despite being disabled Tom works hard for Mr Link Deas.
- He's compassionate and tries to help Mayella.
- He apologises for repeating bad language in court, saying it's "not fittin' for these folks's chillun to hear".
- Mayella's advances towards him are completely unwelcome, but he tries to be as gentle as possible with her — he says he "didn't wanta push her or nothin'".
- He doesn't say anything bad about the Ewells, even after he hears the lies they tell about him in the courtroom.
- Harper Lee presents Tom and his family positively to show how unfair it is that even the very best black families are still seen as below the very worst white families.

Tom is...

polite: his "manners were as good as Atticus's"

caring: "I was glad to do it, Mr Ewell didn't seem to help her none"

hardworking: "I works pretty steady... all year round"

Writer's Techniques

Harper Lee mentions that Tom was jailed for fighting — he's not perfect. This makes him a more believable character.

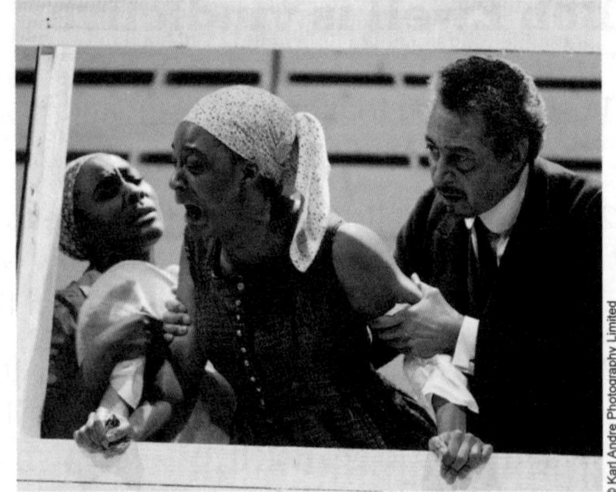

Helen Robinson has to cope with a lot

1) Reverend Sykes organises a church collection to help the Robinsons out financially — he tells the congregation that Helen can't go out to work when Tom's in jail as she can't leave the children home alone.
2) But the real reason that Helen is struggling is the accusation against Tom — people don't want to have anything to do with his family because of what the Ewells say he's done, so nobody will give Helen a job.
3) She is devastated when she hears that Tom has been killed — "she just fell down in the dirt".
4) As if losing her husband isn't bad enough, the Ewells continue to persecute Helen when she has to pass their house to get to work. Bob Ewell follows her and frightens her.

Write about how Tom's fate demonstrates racial prejudice...

It's clear to the reader that the Robinsons are far better people than the Ewells, but most of the jury couldn't put aside their prejudices and make a fair decision. This sort of injustice was rife in America in the 1930s.

Character Profile — Maycomb's Men

It's all well and good knowing about the major families, but you'll just look silly if you get the minor characters mixed up.

Heck Tate tries to keep the peace

© Karl Andre Photography Limited

1) Heck Tate is the sheriff. He goes to the Ewell house when Bob Ewell accuses Tom of rape.
2) He also has to act as a witness for the prosecution but he just tells the court what happened as he saw it, without prejudice.
3) He worries about Tom Robinson's safety and warns Atticus that there might be trouble when he's moved back to Maycomb jail.
4) He's compassionate — when he investigates Bob Ewell's death he understands that Boo, with his "shy ways", wouldn't like the attention he'd get if the real story came out. Heck insists that Bob Ewell fell on his knife and killed himself.

Mr B.B. Underwood runs the Maycomb Tribune

1) Mr Underwood's newspaper offices are near the county jail. He keeps an eye on Atticus when the mob surrounds him at the jail and has him "covered" with his shotgun — he wouldn't have let the mob hurt Atticus and Tom.
2) Strangely, Mr Underwood is a racist — Atticus says he "despises Negroes" — but he respects Atticus and hates injustice.
3) Mr Underwood doesn't like seeing how unfairly Tom has been treated. He writes an editorial after Tom's death saying that "it was a sin to kill cripples". He also compares the shooting of Tom to the senseless killing of songbirds.

Judge John Taylor does the best he can for Tom

Judge Taylor shows his support for Tom Robinson in subtle ways:

- He chooses Atticus to defend Tom when the job would normally have gone to another lawyer. He thinks Atticus is the only lawyer who would be able to give Tom the best shot at justice.
- Judge Taylor doesn't like Bob Ewell — he treats him like he's a total idiot in court.
- He gives a fair summing up of the case for the jury. Reverend Sykes says he even thinks Judge Taylor might have been "leanin' a little to our side" (i.e. Tom Robinson's side).
- Bob Ewell realises that Judge Taylor was on Tom Robinson's side — he tries to get revenge by breaking into Judge Taylor's house.

"Let the dead bury the dead this time, Mr Finch."

Heck says that he's "not a very good man", but he's trying to protect Boo — sounds like a decent guy to me. Lee seems to prefer men to women — apart from Bob Ewell, her men tend to be nicer than her women.

Character Profile — Maycomb's Women

Two very different women who both have a big impact on Jem and Scout are their neighbours, Miss Maudie Atkinson and Mrs Henry Lafayette Dubose.

Miss Maudie is a good neighbour to the children

1) Miss Maudie is an old friend of the Finch family — she admires Atticus and teases Uncle Jack.
2) She's protective of Scout and is a good role model — she's supportive when the ladies make fun of Scout at the missionary tea.
3) She answers the children's questions honestly and never patronises them or tells on them.
4) Scout thinks of her as their friend and tells her one day that she is the "best lady I know".

Miss Maudie is...

fair: "She loved everything that grew in God's earth"
witty: "she had an acid tongue in her head"
sensitive: "She never laughed at me unless I meant to be funny."

Miss Maudie is a wise woman

- Miss Maudie is one of the few adults in the book who is unprejudiced and doesn't involve herself in gossip. She tells Scout early on that Boo Radley is harmless, and that the rumours about him aren't true.
- She admires what Atticus is doing — she says that when the people of Maycomb are called on to do right, they have people like Atticus to do it for them.
- She has a balanced view of religion — she's a Baptist but she doesn't agree with the "foot-washing" Baptists who think "anything that's pleasure is a sin".

Mrs Dubose is a different story

1) Scout thinks Mrs Dubose is the "meanest old woman who ever lived" and describes her as "plain hell". She's scared of her and Jem is too.
2) Mrs Dubose is old and ill and spends her time in bed or in a wheelchair on her front porch — from where she tells the children off whenever they pass.
3) She makes Jem read to her as a punishment for cutting the heads off her camellias.
4) After she dies, the children learn that Mrs Dubose was a morphine addict and was determined to kick her habit. Atticus explains to Jem how much courage she had and says she was "the bravest person I ever knew".

Theme — Innocence and Bravery

The chapter with Mrs Dubose is next to the one with the mad dog incident — Harper Lee is trying to encourage the reader to think about different kinds of bravery.

Character Profile — Maycomb's Women

At Aunt Alexandra's missionary circle tea party, Scout thinks to herself that she prefers men to women because men aren't hypocrites. And with ladies like these as neighbours, who can blame her...

Stephanie Crawford loves a good gossip

Photograph by Leigh Toldi

1) Miss Stephanie Crawford likes to portray herself as someone who goes about the neighbourhood "doing good", but it's pretty clear that she's not very nice.
2) Everyone knows that Stephanie Crawford is a gossip — "no one with a grain of sense trusted" her.
3) She's partly to blame for the false rumours about Boo Radley — she claimed that he looked in through the window at her.
4) She enjoys saying things in front of the children that she knows might upset them. It's Miss Stephanie's "pleasure" to tell Scout and Jem of the threats Bob Ewell has made against their father — she isn't very sensitive.

Mrs Merriweather presents herself as a true Christian

But in reality she's a bit of a hypocrite:

Mrs Merriweather is believed to have sobered up her husband to make a "reasonably useful citizen" out of him.

But the book suggests she has a drinking problem herself — it's not unusual "if Mrs Grace Merriweather sips gin".

She's considered to be the "most devout lady in Maycomb".

Her behaviour isn't very Christian — she thinks about sacking her black servant girl for looking "sulky" after the trial.

She wants to help the Mruna tribe in Africa because they live in "sin and squalor".

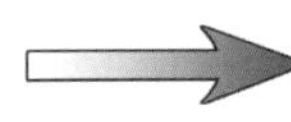

But she's not prepared to help the black families on her own doorstep.

Miss Gates seems a nice woman but has a blind spot

1) Miss Gates is Scout's third-grade teacher — she teaches her class about Hitler's persecution of Jews. She says that in America they "don't believe in persecuting anybody".
2) Miss Gates thinks that persecution is a terrible thing — but Scout overhears her saying that the verdict of Tom Robinson's trial was the right result because it was time somebody "taught 'em a lesson". Miss Gates is a hypocrite and is unable to recognise her own racial prejudices.

"Well, I always say forgive and forget, forgive and forget."

These ladies would faint if you called them hypocrites, but I'm afraid that's what the missionary ladies and Miss Gates are. Their prejudices are so much a part of their society that they can't even recognise them.

Character Profile — Country People

The farmers and country folk of Maycomb County are mainly shown to be decent people.

Mr Link Deas looks after the Robinsons

1) Mr Link Deas is a cotton farmer. He's Tom Robinson's boss and obviously thinks a lot of him.
2) He stands up and vouches for Tom's good character in front of everybody in the courtroom.
3) He gives Helen a job after Tom has been killed, when other employers want nothing to do with her.
4) He stops Bob Ewell from harassing Helen by threatening to charge him with assault.

Mr Dolphus Raymond doesn't fit into Maycomb society

1) Mr Dolphus Raymond owns a lot of land and comes from a respected Maycomb family, but he doesn't behave like other white people — there's a lot of gossip about him because he's different.
2) Everyone thinks that Mr Raymond is a drunk, but Dill discovers "it's nothing but Coca-Cola" that he drinks. He pretends it's whisky so people can blame his drunkenness for the fact that he prefers the company of black people — he thinks that they wouldn't understand otherwise.
3) He trusts Scout and Dill because he knows they're too young to have been corrupted by the prejudice of Maycomb. He's kind to them and clearly has a lot of respect for Atticus.

The Cunninghams turn up all over Maycomb

1) The Cunninghams are poor but respectable people — they "never took anything they can't pay back".
2) Mr Cunningham is in the lynch mob that surrounds Atticus outside the jail. He's brought to his senses when Scout recognises him and innocently chats to him about his son and his legal problems. He then changes his mind and gets all the others to leave.
3) Atticus thinks that Mr Cunningham is basically a good man — he "just has his blind spots".
4) There's also a Cunningham on the jury and he tries to acquit Tom. Atticus says that once you earn their respect, the Cunninghams support you no matter what — "they were for you tooth and nail".

Photograph by Leigh Toldi

Although the Cunninghams are poor and uneducated — like the Ewells — they are also hardworking and respectable. Harper Lee wanted to show that not all the impoverished families are racist and ignorant.

Look at how Lee presents different sectors of society...

The country folk are judged as being poor and ignorant, but if anything they're more open-minded than the supposedly more civilised townspeople. Lee suggests that all people, regardless of their class, are flawed.

Character Profile — Other Characters

Harper Lee's story isn't just about its main characters — it's about the whole town of Maycomb, so it's important to take notice of the minor characters as well as the Finches and Tom Robinson.

Don't forget about background characters like these

All of these people contribute to the story in some way:

Mr Avery Mr Avery lives across the road. The children see him sitting on his porch sneezing each night, and once, memorably, spot him weeing. He helps when Miss Maudie's house catches fire, almost getting stuck climbing through the window. He's also the inspiration for Scout and Jem's "morphodite" snowman.

Miss Caroline Fisher She's Scout's first-grade teacher. She's new to Maycomb and doesn't understand its ways, and she gets cross when Scout tries to help her. She has new (and rather nonsensical) ideas about how children should learn to read and write, and tries to ban Scout from doing so at home. She is clearly unhappy at the end of Scout's first day, but they've got off to such a bad start that Scout doesn't feel sorry for her.

Little Chuck Little He's in Scout's class at school. He's another very poor child, but "a born gentleman" — he's very kind and sweet to Miss Caroline and gets her a cup of water to calm her nerves after she's frightened by the lice in Burris Ewell's hair. He's only little but he's brave and stands up to Burris Ewell.

Cecil Jacobs Another boy at school, who announces in the school yard that "Scout Finch's daddy defended niggers". Scout wants to fight him but because of her promise to Atticus she walks away (for the first time in her life) and is called a coward.

Mr Gilmer He's the lawyer who has the easy job of prosecuting Tom Robinson. He's not as polite or fair in court as Atticus — his harsh cross-examination of Tom makes Dill cry.

Photograph by Leigh Toldi

Mr Gilmer

Dr Reynolds He's the town doctor. Scout is surprised that he knows Arthur Radley, but then realises that Boo must get ill and need a doctor's help sometimes too. He seems to be a kind man and reassures Scout that Jem will be fine after he has his arm broken by Bob Ewell.

Talk about how Lee creates three-dimensional characters...

Lee always mentions a couple of eccentric characteristics to help bring her characters to life. Whether it's the snake in Aunt Rachel Haverford's closet or Judge Taylor's cigar-chewing, they're always memorable.

Practice Questions

Well, they don't ask much of you, do they? Only to get to know an entire fictional town. Try the questions below to find out how well you really know the inhabitants of Maycomb. Trust me, if you don't understand the characters you won't have a chance of doing well in the exam.

Quick Questions

1) Which of the following lists of words best describes Scout Finch?
   a) sensitive, fair, calm
   b) innocent, headstrong, inquisitive
   c) clever, shy, dreamy

2) Find two examples from the text that show Atticus isn't always perfect.

3) Give two examples of events from the book which suggest Jem doesn't always do what he's told.

4) Find a quote from the text that shows that Aunt Alexandra is a bit of a snob.

5) Dill says that he wants to be a clown when he grows up. What does this tell you about his character?

6) Give two examples of how Calpurnia provides a link to the black community for the Finches.

7) Why does Nathan Radley put cement in the knothole of the tree?

8) Give a reason why the reader might feel sorry for Mayella Ewell.

9) Why is Bob Ewell so resentful after he wins the court case?

10) List three examples which show that Tom Robinson is a respectable character.

Practice Questions

Time for some more questions. Don't skip over them because you think they look a bit tough. If you practise your writing skills now, it won't be nearly so bad at exam time.

In-depth Questions

1) Briefly explain how Harper Lee shows the character of Jem growing up in *To Kill a Mockingbird.*
2) How does Aunt Alexandra's character change over the course of the novel?
3) What does Dill running away from home tell you about his character and his relationship with the Finches?
4) Which female character do you think is the best role model for Scout and why?
5) What reason might Harper Lee have for presenting Tom Robinson as such a likeable character?

Exam-style Questions

1) Scout says Atticus didn't "do anything that could possibly arouse the admiration of anyone". How much do you agree?
2) Read the passage from the beginning of Chapter 20 to "that's the way I want to live." How does Harper Lee present Dolphus Raymond in this extract?
3) Describe how Lee presents Mrs Dubose and explain her importance to the novel.
4) The children in the novel are the only characters free of prejudice. How much do you agree?

Racism and Intolerance

This is a monster of a theme — it's the main focus of the novel and one of the main reasons it was written. Lee was influenced by the changing attitudes to racism during the Civil Rights Movement in the 1950s.

Most white people in Maycomb think black people are inferior

1) Racism was rife in the American South during the 1930s — Maycomb is no exception. Prejudice is a normal part of life for most of the characters.
2) The characters don't think twice about using racist language like "darky" or "nigger" — Scout tells Atticus that's "what everybody at school says".
3) They're misinformed and ignorant about black people — the missionary ladies believe that Africa is full of "sin and squalor".
4) The white community don't have any respect for the black community — the white men gamble in the black community's church during the week.
5) Atticus calls racism Maycomb's "usual disease". The word "usual" shows just how common racism is, and how hard it'll be to change what so many people have believed all their lives.

Writer's Techniques

When characters use racist language like this they don't think it's offensive. They think that black people are inferior and don't need to be treated with respect.

It's not easy to stand up against racism

1) Atticus realises he's "licked" before the trial even starts — the court won't take the word of a black man over the word of a white man, even if that white man is "trash" like Bob Ewell.
2) People's prejudices are even stronger than cold, hard evidence — Atticus proves that Tom couldn't have attacked Mayella because of his crippled left arm, but despite this the jury still find Tom guilty.
3) The people of Maycomb aren't afraid to show their feelings about the trial — they call Atticus a "nigger-lover" and Scout and Jem have to put up with insults from both children and adults.
4) Defending Tom Robinson makes Atticus vulnerable to violence too — he's threatened by a lynch mob and by Bob Ewell.

Historical Background

Tom Robinson's trial is similar to the real-life Scottsboro Trials in 1931. Have a look at p.3 and familiarise yourself with what happened during this trial. You can pick up marks for showing you're aware of the historical context of the book.

Racism and Intolerance

Things may be starting to change a little by the end

1) The jury takes several hours to reach a verdict — and one jury member argues that Tom Robinson is innocent. Miss Maudie says that this is a "baby-step" towards a more equal and tolerant society.
2) Mr Link Deas gives Tom's wife a job and stands up for her when Bob Ewell tries to frighten her.
3) Aunt Alexandra is horrified by Tom's death — she's begun to realise the consequences of Maycomb's prejudices.
4) But many people in Maycomb still see black people as second class citizens:

- The jury find Tom guilty even though it's obvious he's innocent.
- The missionary ladies think that Atticus has stirred up trouble by defending Tom.
- Maycomb loses interest in Tom's death after two days — his death is insignificant to them.

Racism isn't the only type of intolerance in the novel

Aside from racism, Harper Lee refers to three other types of intolerance in her novel:

Social Intolerance

- Aunt Alexandra won't let Scout play with Walter Cunningham because his family are poor — she doesn't think the Cunninghams are good enough for the Finches.
- Dolphus Raymond has to pretend to be a drunk in order to get people to accept the fact he prefers the company of black people. There's more on social intolerance on p.51.

Gender Intolerance

- There's sexism in Maycomb — Miss Maudie tells Scout that "foot-washers think women are a sin by definition", and women aren't allowed to sit on a jury.
- Aunt Alexandra is always trying to turn Scout into a lady — she won't let Scout wear her dungarees because they're not very ladylike.
- It's not just the women who are expected to behave in a certain way — Dill's parents tell him: "Boys get out and play baseball with the other boys".

Gender intolerance means discriminating against someone because they're male or female.

Religious Intolerance

- "foot-washing" Baptists tell Miss Maudie she's going to hell just because she grows flowers.
- People gossip about the Radley family because they don't go to church and worship at home.

Comment on the different types of intolerance in Maycomb...

The number of things Maycomb people can find to disapprove of is amazing — growing flowers, wearing dungarees, defending innocent men, and even staying in your own house... No wonder Boo stays inside.

Empathy

Empathy comes up time and again throughout the novel — even if you don't like a character, Harper Lee encourages you to try and understand them better.

Empathy is really important

1) Empathising with someone means being able to understand why they act the way they do. This is what Atticus means when he talks about standing in someone else's shoes.
2) Lee makes it very obvious how important empathy is — Atticus talks about the importance of seeing things from someone else's perspective four times in the novel.
3) Harper Lee wanted to show that teaching people to empathise with others reduces the chances of them being prejudiced.

The people of Maycomb aren't too great at empathy

Harper Lee tries to show that there are different reasons for a lack of empathy.

- The children — especially Scout — tend not to be empathetic because of their youth. For example, Atticus has to teach Scout to see things from Miss Caroline's perspective after her disastrous first day at school.
- Some of the characters lack empathy because of their prejudices. Racist characters like Bob Ewell or Mrs Merriweather don't empathise with the black community because they don't think black people matter as much as white people.
- But there are characters who are able to see past their prejudices. Mr Underwood "despises Negroes" but he's able to recognise the unfairness of Tom's death and writes an article about Tom's "senseless slaughter".
- Harper Lee suggests that children who aren't taught about the importance of empathy will grow up to be as prejudiced as previous generations — Francis uses terms like "nigger-lover" because the adults around him use them. Characters like Francis don't give the reader hope that things will change in the future.

The reader is supposed to empathise with certain characters

1) The reader empathises with Scout and Jem from the very start of the book because they're likeable characters who bring humour to the novel.
2) You start off disliking some characters, such as Mayella Ewell, but then you realise that there's another side to them. Harper Lee persuades the reader to feel sorry for Mayella by showing that she's overworked, abused and neglected. You can't excuse her behaviour but you can try to understand it.
3) But Lee makes it equally clear that she doesn't want the reader to empathise with Bob Ewell — she does this by not giving him any redeeming qualities.

You can tell how important the idea of understanding other people is, because it's the last thing Atticus talks about in the book. He says that most people are nice "when you finally see them"

"you never really know a man until you stand in his shoes"

If you're writing about empathy, think about the reader as well as how the characters behave towards one another. For example, Lee wants us to empathise with the Finches, but not with Bob Ewell.

Childhood and Growing Up

Scout, Jem and Dill don't seem to have quite as much fun as they become more grown up — but they do gain a better understanding of the world around them.

One of the book's main themes is growing up

1) *To Kill a Mockingbird* is a bildungsroman. This is a type of book which focuses on characters who grow up and learn lessons about life — just like Scout and Jem do.
2) Because Lee tells the story through a child's eyes the reader sees how simple the relationships between children are. For example, after Scout beats up Walter Cunningham in the schoolyard she ends up inviting him to lunch — unlike the adults of Maycomb the children don't hold grudges — they're quick to forgive and forget.

The trial forces the children to grow up

1) At the start of the book there's lots of description of childhood friendships, games and dares — this shows how young and innocent the children are.
2) But as time passes there's less focus on playtime and games and more focus on the things that happen to the children which force them to grow up — like the trial.
3) Although both Jem and Scout grow up quite a bit by the end of the novel, it's Jem who matures the most. Scout mentions several times about how her and Jem "began to part company".
4) It's not just Scout who recognises that Jem is maturing. Miss Maudie lets Jem have a slice of the adults' cake and Cal starts calling him "Mister". There's more about Jem growing up on p.30.

But Lee wants to show how important innocence is

- Scout's innocent chatter with Mr Cunningham outside the jail stops the lynch mob from attacking and her childish costume protects her from Bob Ewell's knife — Harper Lee wants to show how powerful innocence can be.
- Lee makes sure that Scout doesn't become bitter or cynical because of what happens to her. At the end of the novel she falls asleep on Atticus's knee. This kind of behaviour reminds the reader that she's still a child.

There's more on the theme of innocence on p.52.

Cynical means seeing the worst in things.

"There wasn't much else left for us to learn..."

"...except possibly algebra." Scout's still a child — she doesn't realise that she's actually got lots left to learn in life. Though I don't know why she's so bothered about algebra — I've never found it particularly useful...

Education

Scout and Jem learn a lot over the course of the novel, but not much of that learning happens at school...

Harper Lee makes fun of formal education

Satirising something means making fun of people or ideas by exaggerating them to make them seem ridiculous.

1) Harper Lee satirises classroom learning, for example when Scout's teacher, Miss Caroline, finds out she can read and write, she punishes her rather than encouraging her.
2) Another of Scout's teachers, Miss Gates, is a hypocrite — she teaches the children that Hitler's persecution of Jews is wrong, but supports the persecution of black people in her own neighbourhood.
3) Although Harper Lee makes fun of school she makes it very clear that education is important. Uneducated characters who don't go to school, like the Ewells, come across as ignorant.

The children learn more outside the classroom

1) Most of the story happens during the summer holidays or after school — this helps Lee to show how much the children learn outside the classroom.
2) At the start of the novel Scout thinks that Atticus "hasn't taught me anything" — but over the course of the novel he gives Scout a moral education. He teaches her about empathy, courage and fairness.
3) It's not just Atticus that the children learn from — Calpurnia teaches Scout manners, Miss Maudie teaches the children to respect their father and Aunt Alexandra teaches Scout how to be a lady.
4) Other characters learn valuable lessons too.

- Mr Cunningham is educated by Scout outside the jail, when her friendly chatter helps him to realise that wanting to harm Tom Robinson is wrong.
- Aunt Alexandra is initially against Atticus defending Tom, but when he loses the trial she seems genuinely sorry. It's as if she's starting to see that Atticus may be right in some ways.

Harper Lee shows how powerful education can be

Being repressed means not having the freedom or opportunities that other people have.

1) Well-educated characters like Atticus and Uncle Jack are portrayed as powerful — people respect them. They're good, fair-minded characters.
2) It's hard for the black characters to get an education because the black children aren't allowed to go to school with the white children. Without an education they're powerless — they can't get any jobs other than manual labour.

Theme — Racism

Segregated education is another example of how black people are repressed by the white community.

3) But characters like Calpurnia give the reader hope — she can read and has taught her son Zeebo how to read too. This suggests that passing on education is important to the black community's future.

Write about how education is linked to tolerance...

Although Lee makes fun of classroom learning, you can write about how she's making a serious point underneath it all — that misunderstanding and a lack of education are often at the root of intolerance.

Family and Social Class

Everybody knows everybody in Maycomb — that's small towns for you.
You sneeze, and before you know it, everyone's talking about it for weeks.

It's impossible to escape your family background

1) Scout says that the families in the town have lived together for so long, they have become "utterly predictable to one another" — this means that people are expected to behave in a certain way. For example, everyone knows Stephanie Crawford has a gossiping "streak".
2) These streaks can pass on from generation to generation. For example, Burris Ewell is filthy and rude — when the reader is introduced to the rest of his family they're no different.
3) The fact that children will grow up to be like their parents suggests that prejudices will also be passed on.
4) It's almost impossible to be viewed as an individual rather than part of a family. When the town discovers Atticus will be defending a black man they don't just take it out on him — they insult Jem and Scout too.

Social prejudice is everywhere in Maycomb

1) There's a social hierarchy in Maycomb — relatively wealthy families like the Finches are at the top, poorer families like the Cunninghams are below, the Ewells towards the bottom, and the black community at the very bottom.
2) Aunt Alexandra thinks family reputation is really important — she's a bit of a snob. She doesn't think that Walter Cunningham is good enough to play with Scout.
3) Scout has a different understanding of good breeding to Aunt Alexandra. She thinks it's about making the best out of the sense you have, so she's confused when Aunt Alexandra tells her she can't play with Walter, even though one of his family thought Tom was innocent.

Some people don't fit into their family

1) Dill is sent away to Miss Rachel's every summer and he doesn't have a father. He says his family aren't interested in him and don't need him.
2) Boo Radley is kept inside for years by his family because he got in with the wrong crowd as a teenager.
3) Mayella Ewell grows red geraniums and unlike the rest of her family tries to keep herself clean. But because Maycomb think the rest of her family are "trash" they assume she must be too.
4) By the end of the novel Scout and Jem want to fit into their family — Jem wants to be a lawyer like Atticus and Scout recognises the "skill" in being a lady. But they also want to be fair and respectful because Atticus has shown them that this is important.

Photograph by Leigh Todd

"Jean Louise will not invite Walter Cunningham to this house"

Aunt Alexandra is obsessed with family reputation, but she's not the only one. Remember, Maycomb has a family hierarchy as well as a racial hierarchy — you're judged by your name before anything else. Bit harsh.

Innocence and Bravery

'Innocence' doesn't just mean 'not being guilty of something' — it can also mean 'being gentle, harmless and seeing the goodness in everything'. You might call it inner sense...

There are lots of innocent people in Maycomb...

1) Lee shows in *To Kill a Mockingbird* how it's impossible to be completely innocent forever — Scout and Jem become less innocent as they grow up because of the things they experience.
2) This loss of innocence isn't always a bad thing — sometimes Scout's innocence and naivety put her in danger. For example, when she stands up to the lynch mob, it's clear she doesn't understand the risk she's taking.
3) Characters like Tom Robinson and Boo Radley also show that innocence can be dangerous. It was Tom's innocence and good nature that led to him being accused by the Ewells and Boo puts his own life at risk when he tries to help the children.
4) The 'good' characters in the book, like Atticus, keep some of the qualities we associate with innocence — such as a desire to always look for the good in people.

The mockingbird is a symbol of innocence in the book — for a bit of info about who the story's 'mockingbirds' are, turn to p.59.

... and lots of brave people too

The story shows that you don't have to be strong or aggressive to be brave.

1) Mrs Dubose is brave, because she puts herself through so much pain to die free of her morphine addiction.
2) Atticus uses Mrs Dubose as a way of explaining to the children that bravery is when "you know you're licked before you begin but you begin anyway and you see it through no matter what".
3) Atticus is brave in a similar way to Mrs Dubose — he knows when he agrees to defend Tom Robinson that he can't win but he's brave because he tries anyway.
4) He also stands up for what he believes is right even though so many people disagree with him. Even the mob at the jail can't succeed in intimidating him.
5) Mr Underwood is brave to write the article about Tom's death because he knows that most people will disagree. Link Deas is brave too — he vouches for Tom in court and protects Helen from Bob Ewell.

"I wanted you to see what real courage is"

Atticus explains that real bravery means fighting for what's right, even if sometimes you're going to end up losing. And here was me thinking that bravery was managing not to cry like a baby on trips to the dentist.

Practice Questions

Oh great, time for more practice questions. Well actually, they are great, because they'll help you realise where the gaps are in your understanding of the novel. As a bonus feature, they'll also get you thinking about your opinions on the novel and its themes.

Quick Questions

1) Harper Lee calls racism Maycomb's "usual disease" — what does this phrase tell you about attitudes towards race in Maycomb?

2) Give two examples of events that suggest that some people's racist attitudes might be beginning to change.

3) Why does Dolphus Raymond pretend to be a drunk?

4) How does Harper Lee encourage the reader to empathise with Mayella Ewell?

5) What is a 'bildungsroman'?

6) Why does Miss Caroline tell Scout off?

7) What has Aunt Alexandra learnt by the end of *To Kill a Mockingbird*?

8) Why doesn't Aunt Alexandra want Scout to play with Walter Cunningham?

9) Give an example from the novel where Harper Lee suggests that innocence can be dangerous.

10) Explain briefly why Mrs Dubose is brave.

Practice Questions

Here are a few more questions for you to embrace with enthusiasm. Yes, enthusiasm. Well, OK, just try not to look too bored. You'll be glad you had a go at writing essay answers when the exam comes round, I promise. And don't forget to mention the novel's historical context if you can — it'll score you big marks on the day.

In-depth Questions

1) List three types of intolerance in Maycomb other than racism and give examples from the book to support each of them.

2) Does Harper Lee portray innocence as a good or a bad thing? Back up your answer with examples from the novel.

3) Scout and Jem learn a lot during *To Kill a Mockingbird.* Do you think they learn more in school or outside the classroom? Explain your answer.

4) Which character in the book do you think is the bravest? Give a reason for your answer.

Exam-style Questions

1) How far do you think racist attitudes in Maycomb are beginning to change by the end of the novel?

2) Read the passage in Chapter 31 from "I was beginning to learn" to "Radley porch was enough". How does Lee present Scout's ability to empathise with others in this passage?

3) How does Harper Lee present the theme of family in the novel?

4) To what extent has Scout lost her innocence by the end of the novel?

Narrative and Suspense in 'To Kill A Mockingbird'

Harper Lee uses narrative tricks and techniques to keep the reader interested. The way the story is told creates suspense and adds to the drama of the narrative.

Scout is the narrator of the story

For more on the children's language turn to p.56.

1) The whole story is narrated by Scout. She's an adult when she tells the story but it's from the point of view of Scout as a child.
2) Older Scout's language is more sophisticated than younger Scout's. The dialogue shows the reader what younger Scout's language is like — it's generally childish and simple.
3) Writing the book as a first-person narrative allows Harper Lee to achieve several things:
    - realism — the reader watches the children grow up. This makes the book more believable and helps the reader to empathise with the children.
    - an adult perspective — older Scout can reflect on things that have happened — this allows Harper Lee to give an adult view of younger Scout's actions.
4) Writing the novel from the point of view of a child also allows Harper Lee to create:
    - humour and irony — when Scout misunderstands something it's charming and comical. This provides some light relief after the more serious bits of the book.
    - an innocent perspective — the reader sees prejudice through the eyes of a child who doesn't understand it. This helps to show how wrong prejudice is and makes the reader more likely to accept the book's message.
5) Scout can be an unreliable narrator — she sometimes gives inaccurate descriptions of people and events, such as her description of Boo Radley. This is deliberate because Harper Lee wants to show the risk of not forming your own opinions.

Harper Lee uses suspense to keep the reader interested

1) Lee sometimes holds information back to create suspense — in Chapter 21 the children go home for dinner while the jury are out. The reader, like the children, is anxious to return to the courtroom for the verdict.
2) It takes almost the whole book for Boo Radley to be revealed, and at the end it's ages before you know for sure that it was Boo who saved the children.
3) Harper Lee also uses foreshadowing to create tension. Foreshadowing is when the book hints at something that happens later such as Aunt Alexandra's feeling of apprehension before Bob attacks the children.
4) Things are often hinted at — e.g. when Harper Lee hints that Bob Ewell abuses Mayella. She does this so you form your own opinions about what happens in the book.
5) The main plot line doesn't end happily — Tom is shot dead trying to escape from prison. This makes the story more realistic and less predictable.

Comment on why Harper Lee uses Scout as the narrator...

Scout seems a bit confused sometimes, but it's just a trick to add some humour and light-hearted moments to the book. You can also talk about the way that her narrative makes the novel seem more realistic.

Language in 'To Kill a Mockingbird'

To Kill a Mockingbird is a modern classic, respected by all kinds of clever literary types — but that definitely doesn't mean that everyone in it speaks in a posh way and uses big words.

Harper Lee uses Southern speech to set the scene

1) Harper Lee uses dialogue to mimic the way people would've talked in 1930s Alabama. She makes it realistic by using:

- dialect words — she uses some unfamiliar Southern words like "scuppernong" (a type of grape) or "shinny" (a type of alcohol).
- non-standard spelling — Harper Lee tries to suggest how words would've been pronounced by spelling words differently such as "pizened" for "poisoned" and "chillun" for "children".
- ellipsis — letters are missed off words and replaced with an apostrophe to show how the words would've sounded such as "goin'", "nothin'", "makin'"

2) Harper Lee uses Southern dialogue like this for the same reasons she describes Maycomb in such detail (see p.9) — she wants to make it clear that although the story is fictional, the events of the novel could've happened in any Southern town in the 1930s.

The children's language is a lot more casual

1) The children's language is more chatty than the adults' way of talking — they use childish language e.g. slang like "cooties" (head lice) and insults such as "Cecil Jacobs is a big fat hen".
2) They use hyperbole and imaginative language — Scout says that Atticus knew "everything" and Jem describes Boo as having "yellow and rotten" teeth.

Hyperbole is the technical term for when a writer exaggerates something.

3) But they are often respectful when they talk to adults. They often use full titles like "Miss Maudie" and "Mrs Merriweather" and when they're talking to Atticus they often call him "sir" — this reflects the polite manners of the South at the time.
4) The children sometimes don't understand the words they use e.g. Scout asks Uncle Jack, "What's a whore-lady?" — this shows the reader how innocent they still are.

The black community talk differently

1) In the book, black people and white people have different dialects and the black community uses less standard grammar — e.g. "They's my comp'ny", "I wants to know". This reflects their lack of education.
2) In Chapter 12 Scout tells Cal that "nigger-talk" isn't right — this is a good example of how white characters assume anything they do is better than anything black people do.

Language in 'To Kill a Mockingbird'

People's characters are revealed by how they speak

1) Atticus is respectful to everyone. At the trial he calls Mayella, "Ma'am". She assumes he must be mocking her because she isn't used to politeness.
2) Tom Robinson challenges the white characters' stereotypical views of black men — he's very thoughtful and polite. He calls Atticus "suh" and feels uncomfortable repeating bad language in court.
3) Bob Ewell talks in an aggressive and nasty way — this reflects his character. During the trial he uses coarse language like "ruttin'" and "screamin' like a stuck hog".

Photograph by Leigh Toldi

The characters' language reveals a lot about their status

1) The less-educated characters like the Ewells, Cunninghams and the black community have stronger accents than the more educated townspeople like Atticus and Miss Maudie.
2) Aunt Alexandra uses the word "aren't" while the children use "ain't" — she's much more concerned about her image and sounding correct.
3) Calpurnia changes how she speaks depending on whether she's talking to black or white people — she knows that she wouldn't fit into the black community if she spoke to them like she does to the Finches. Cal understands how important language is to her identity.

There's some sensitive language in the book

1) A lot of the white characters call black people "niggers". In the 1930s most white people wouldn't have seen this as being offensive.
2) When Scout is young, she says "nigger" because all her schoolmates do. Atticus tells her not to say it because it's "common" — he uses the more respectful word "Negro".
3) The older Scout who narrates the novel uses the more acceptable word "Negro" — this shows how she's learnt some sensitivity.

Be careful when you're writing about sensitive language — the word 'nigger' is now seen as a very offensive word.

Historical Context

They're not acceptable today, but when Harper Lee was writing in the 1950s the terms "Negro" and "coloured" would have been in common usage, and weren't thought of as derogatory.

Talk about the effects of Lee's use of dialect...

Lee uses dialect to make her characters sound more authentic, but don't start writing in it unless you're quoting one of the characters — you'll lose marks straightaway if you don't use proper English in the exam.

Language in 'To Kill a Mockingbird'

Harper Lee writes in a really lively, vivid way that's very easy to read. Make sure you learn the different names for the techniques she uses — getting them right will really impress the examiner.

Harper Lee's language is really descriptive

The events described in the book are miles away from most people's experiences nowadays, but Harper Lee uses lots of descriptive techniques to make the unfamiliar more recognisable.

Metaphors

She uses a metaphor to describe the setting — Maycomb is "an island in a patchwork sea of cotton fields and timber land". This metaphor makes it really easy for the reader to imagine what Maycomb looks like.

Simile

When the rabid dog is coming up the street and when the jury are returning to give their verdict, Harper Lee uses the same simile — she describes people moving like "underwater swimmers". This gives the idea of time slowing down at moments of tension or fear.

Personification

She uses personification to make things really come alive — the tin foil in the knothole is described as "winking at me in the afternoon sun" and the Radley's house is said to be "droopy and sick".

Personification is a technique where objects are described using human characteristics.

Imagery

When the children are attacked by Bob Ewell and Scout is blinded by her costume, Harper Lee uses lots of sensory imagery to describe what's happening — "My toes touched trousers" and "I smelled stale whisky". This heightens the tension because the reader isn't sure what's happening.

Harper Lee uses figurative language to describe her characters

1) Harper Lee gives vivid descriptions of the most important characters — this gives the reader a really clear impression of what they're like.
2) When Scout describes Mrs Dubose it's horrifying — her face is "the colour of a dirty pillowcase" and she has "Cords of saliva" on her mouth.
3) Mayella Ewell is described as being like a "steady-eyed cat with a twitchy tail" — it makes the reader think that she's devious and sneaky.
4) Scout describes Aunt Alexandra as being like "Mount Everest" — she's cold and imposing but also long-standing, like the Finch family.
5) Calpurnia is described as having a hand "wide as a bed slat and twice as hard". This suggests she isn't afraid to discipline the children — she's strict and stern.

Photograph by Leigh Toldi

Language in 'To Kill a Mockingbird'

The mockingbird is a symbol of innocence

1) Mockingbirds are mentioned frequently throughout the book — Miss Maudie describes mockingbirds as creatures that "don't do one thing but sing their hearts out for us" and Atticus tells the children that it's a "sin to kill a mockingbird".
2) Harper Lee uses mockingbirds to symbolise innocent creatures that need to be protected from evil. This makes Tom and Boo the novel's most obvious 'mockingbirds' because:
   - they are both victims of prejudice — Tom is a victim of racial prejudice, while Boo is a victim of social prejudice.
   - they are locked up — Tom is locked up in the county jail and Boo is trapped inside his own home by his father and brother.
   - they are innocent — Tom is innocent of raping Mayella, Boo is innocent of his 'monstrous' reputation.
   - they are compassionate — Tom helps Mayella for free, and Boo looks after the children and leaves them gifts.
3) Tom's death is compared to the "senseless slaughter of songbirds" and Scout thinks blaming Boo for Bob Ewell's death would be like "shootin' a mockingbird".
4) Jem could also be seen as the book's mockingbird. He loses his innocence over the course of the novel as he starts to understand how prejudiced the people of Maycomb really are.

Bird names are used quite a lot in the book. There are the Finches and Tom *Robinson* — both small, vulnerable, singing birds. Bob Ewell on the other hand is described as "a little red rooster" and a "bantam cock" — he's compared to a chicken, a flightless bird that 'crows' rather than sings. He doesn't do anything for the benefit of others and is unable to 'fly' above his own prejudices.

Photograph by Leigh Toldi

There are other symbols in the book

The Radley House

The Radley house represents fear and isolation. The children are terrified of the house. The shutters are always closed, showing how nothing is allowed in, or out, of the house.

Nut-grass

Miss Maudie tells the children how nut-grass (a type of weed) "can ruin a whole yard". Nut-grass is a symbol for prejudice which can 'take root' and ruin a town like Maycomb.

The Snowman

After the snowfall in Chapter 8, Jem and Scout build a snowman out of dirt and then cover it in snow. The fact that the snowman is black underneath its thin covering of snow suggests that it's a symbol for how everybody is the same underneath regardless of skin colour.

Write about the different language techniques Lee uses...

Language can be tricky, but it's vital you get to grips with it. No matter what question you pick in the exam, there's always something to say about language. If you can use technical terms, you're bound to impress.

Structure and Form in 'To Kill a Mockingbird'

The language of the book seems quite straightforward — it's simple and direct. But the structure is a bit more complicated — Lee uses it to vary the pace, build tension and keep the reader's attention.

The novel's set over a long period of time

1) The events of *To Kill a Mockingbird* occur over three years and the novel is chronological — the action is described in the order it happens. This makes the narrative easy to follow and allows Harper Lee to build upon themes and messages introduced earlier in the novel.
2) The story is told as a memory — the novel begins with older Scout talking about when Jem broke his arm and ends with Jem in bed with a broken arm. This creates a link between the two parts of the novel.

The novel is split into two parts

Although the main plot-line of the novel — Tom Robinson's trial — doesn't start until Part Two, Part One is al important. The fact that Lee spends almost half the novel describing Scout and Jem's childhood shows how important the theme of innocence is in the novel. It also introduces ideas that are developed in Part Two:

Part One		Part Two
The major characters and some of the minor characters are introduced. This sets the scene and makes the reader familiar with Maycomb.	→	Lee develops her characters and makes them more complex — e.g. we see a new side to Aunt Alexandra after Tom Robinson's death. This make her characters more sophisticated and engaging.
The tone of Part One is quite light-hearted and focuses on the children's summers and their games. Jem and Scout are innocent and mostly untroubled.	→	Jem starts to grow up and this sets a serious tone for the more adult events of the trial. Scout and Jem are exposed to unfairness and prejudice and the children begin to lose their innocence.
Part One takes place over two years — the pace is quite slow and represents life in a sleepy Southern town.	→	Most of the action in Part Two takes place over a few months — this quickens the pace and heightens the drama.
The mockingbird is introduced as a symbol of innocence — the children are told "it's a sin to kill a mockingbird".	→	Mr Underwood compares Tom's death to "the senseless slaughter of songbirds" — continuing the symbolism makes the image more powerful and links events together.
The novel's key themes are introduced, e.g. the theme of courage is introduced by what happens with Mrs Dubose and the mad dog.	→	These early examples of courage prepare the reader for the bravery shown by Atticus and Tom Robinson at Tom's trial.
The unusual snowfall and the fire at the end of Part One create a sense of foreboding.	→	This foreboding foreshadows the unhappy outcome of Tom Robinson's trial.

Foreboding is a feeling that something bad is going to happen.

"He said it began the summer Dill came to us"

The book covers over three years, from the start of the summer when Scout's nearly six to the autumn she's almost nine. I like the way the novel starts and ends with Jem's broken arm — it makes it feel complete.

Practice Questions

Here they are — the very last set of practice questions. You know the drill by now, but don't just rush through them so you can get to the end of the section. If you can't answer the Quick Questions straightaway, flick back through the section to make sure you know your stuff. Spending a bit of time thinking about your answers now will help you loads when it comes to the exam.

Quick Questions

1) Give two advantages of narrating *To Kill a Mockingbird* from a child's perspective.

2) Find an example of foreshadowing from the novel.

3) Find two examples of Southern dialect from the novel.

4) How does Scout and Jem's language differ from the adults' language?

5) Find an example from the novel of Bob Ewell using coarse language.

6) Which character changes how they speak depending on whether they're with black or white people?

7) What does 'personification' mean? Give an example of personification from the book.

8) Harper Lee uses the mockingbird as a symbol in *To Kill a Mockingbird*. Give another example of a symbol used in the novel.

9) In *To Kill a Mockingbird*, is the action described in:
   a) the order it happens?
   b) reverse order?
   c) no set order?

10) Briefly describe how the tone of Part One is different from the tone of Part Two.

Practice Questions

OK, you've warmed up with the shorter questions so it's time to really flex your essay-writing arm. Find your pen and paper and get going on these. They're not fun, but they are useful. Promise.

In-depth Questions

1) Briefly explain why you think Harper Lee decided to narrate *To Kill a Mockingbird* from Scout's perspective.

2) What does Tom Robinson's way of speaking tell us about his character?

3) Find the description of Dill from Chapter One that starts with "Dill was a curiosity..." and ends with "...centre of his forehead". Pick out two examples of figurative language from the passage and say what they tell the reader about Dill.

4) Find an example of each of the following from the text and explain why you think Harper Lee has used them:
   a) metaphor
   b) simile
   c) personification

Exam-style Questions

1) How does the structure of *To Kill a Mockingbird* help to build suspense in the novel?

2) How does Harper Lee suggest that the way characters use language affects the way people treat them?

3) "Boo Radley is the mockingbird referred to in the title of *To Kill a Mockingbird.*" How much do you agree with the above statement?

4) Read the passage in Chapter 31 from "I ran up the steps" to the end. How does Harper Lee use this passage to end the novel in a positive way?

Exam Preparation

Getting to know the text will put you at a massive advantage in the exam. It's not enough just to read it though — you've got to get to grips with the nitty-gritty bits. It's all about gathering evidence...

The exam questions will test four main skills

You will need to show the examiner that you can:

1) Write about the text in a thoughtful way — picking out appropriate examples and quotations to back up your opinions.
2) Identify and explain features of the book's form, structure and language. Show how Lee uses these to present the ideas, themes, characters and settings effectively.
3) Link the story to its cultural, social and historical background (i.e. 1930s America). You need to understand the impact and influence the book has had.
4) Write in a clear, well-structured way. 5% of the marks in your English Literature exams are for spelling, punctuation and grammar. Make sure that your writing is as accurate as possible.

Preparation is important

1) It's important to cover all the different sections of this book in your revision. You need to make sure you understand the text's context, plot, characters, themes and writer's techniques.
2) In the exam, you'll need to bring together your ideas about these topics to answer the question quickly.
3) Think about the different characters and themes in the text, and write down some key points and ideas about each one. Then, find some evidence to support each point — this could be something from any of the sections in this book. You could set out your evidence in a table like this:

Character: Atticus	
Respects other people	"I do my best to love everybody". Earns other people's respect in return — people look up to him.
Good father	Teaches his children important life lessons. Also spends time with them — context: unusual for fathers of the time.
Some faults	Lee gives him flaws to make him more believable, e.g. gets angry and has a "fierce discussion" with Aunt Alexandra.
Fights for justice	Takes on Tom's case even though he knows they'll lose. Sits outside the jail to protect Tom and preserve his right to a trial.
Language	Polite — reflects his unprejudiced approach, e.g. calls Mayella "Ma'am" at the trial even though he thinks she's lying.

Preparing to succeed — a cunning plot indeed...

Knowing the plot inside out will be unbelievably helpful in the exam. It'll help you to stay calm and make sure you write a brilliant answer that positively glitters with little gems of evidence. The exam's just a chance for you to show off...

The Exam Question

This page deals with how to approach an exam question. The stuff below will help you get started on a scorching exam answer, more scorching than, say, a phoenix cooking fiery fajitas in a flaming furnace.

Read the question carefully and underline key words

1) The style of question you'll get depends on which exam board you're taking.
2) Read all the instructions carefully. Make sure you know how many questions you need to answer and how much time you should spend answering each one.
3) If the question has more than one part, look at the total number of marks for each bit. This should help you to plan your time in the exam.
4) Read the question at least twice so you completely understand it. Underline the key words. If you're given an extract, underline important words or phrases in that too.

Henry didn't read the weather report carefully enough when planning his weekend activities.

Here's an exam-style question

Remember to write about form, structure and language.

'How questions' ask you to think about the writer's techniques. E.g. Lee's narrative voice and characterisation.

Q1 How does Lee present the theme of empathy in the novel?
Refer to the following extract in your answer...

Empathy is a key theme — use a range of examples to support your answer.

You must refer to and quote from the extract in your answer.

Some exam boards will ask you to write only about the extract. Others will ask you to write about the extract and the text as a whole. Make sure you read the instructions carefully.

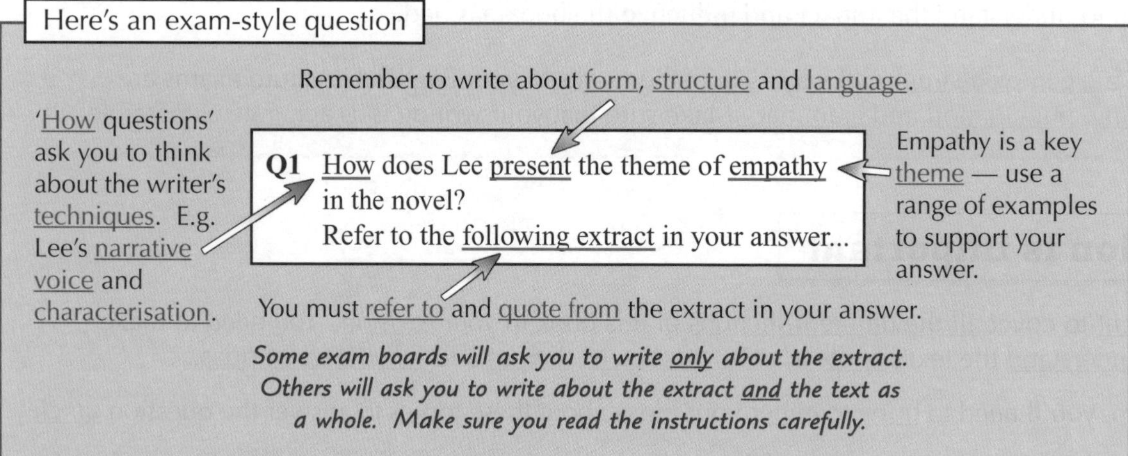

Get to know exam language

Some words come up time and again in exam questions. Have a look at some specimen questions, pick out words that are often used in questions and make sure that you understand what they mean. You could write a few down whilst you're revising. For example:

Question Word	You need to...
Explore / Explain	Show how the writer deals with a theme, character or idea. Make several different points to answer the question.
How does	Think about the techniques or literary features that the author uses to get their point across.
Give examples	Use direct quotes and describe events from the text in your own words.
Refer to	Read the question so that you know if you need to write about just an extract, or an extract and the rest of the text.

The advice squad — the best cops in the NYPD...

Whatever question you're asked in the exam, your answer should touch on the main characters, themes, structure and language of the text. All the stuff we've covered in the rest of the book in fact. It's so neat, it's almost like we planned it.

Planning Your Answer

I'll say this once — and then I'll probably repeat it several times — it is absolutely, completely, totally and utterly essential that you make a plan before you start writing. Only a fool jumps right in without a plan...

Plan your answer before you start

1) If you plan, you're less likely to forget something important.
2) A good plan will help you organise your ideas — and write a good, well-structured essay.
3) Write your plan at the top of your answer booklet and draw a neat line through it when you've finished.
4) Don't spend too long on your plan. It's only rough work, so you don't need to write in full sentences. Here are a few examples of different ways you can plan your answer:

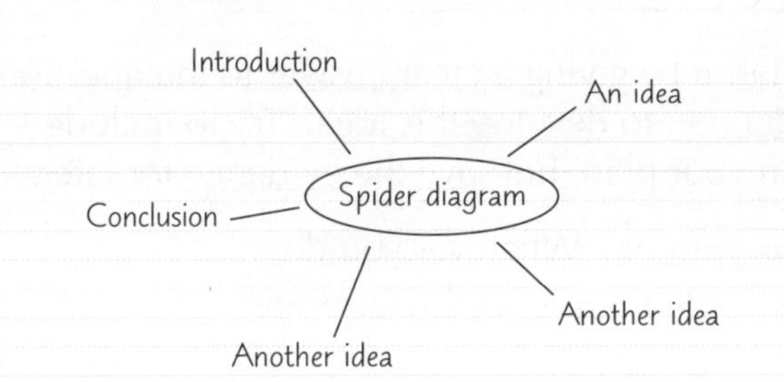

Bullet points...
- Introduction...
- An idea...
- The next idea...
- Another idea...
- Yet another idea...
- Conclusion...

Include bits of evidence in your plan

1) Writing your essay will be much easier if you include important quotes and examples in your plan.
2) You could include them in a table like this one:
3) Don't spend too long writing out quotes though. It's just to make sure you don't forget anything when you write your answer.

A point...	Quote to back this up...
Another point...	Quote...
A different point...	Example...
A brand new point...	Quote...

Structure your answer

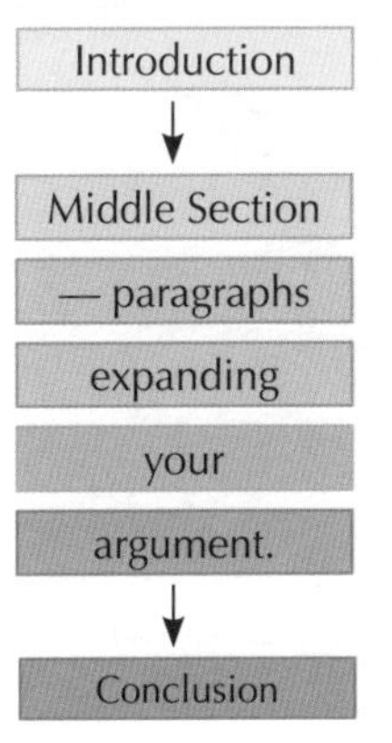

1) Your introduction should give a brief answer to the question you're writing about. Make it clear how you're going to tackle the topic.
2) The middle section of your essay should explain your answer in detail and give evidence to back it up. Write a paragraph for each point you make. Make sure you comment on your evidence and explain how it helps to prove your point.
3) Remember to write a conclusion — a paragraph at the end which sums up your main points. There's more about introductions and conclusions on the next page.

Dirk finally felt ready to tackle the topic.

To plan or not to plan, that is the question...

The answer is yes, yes, a thousand times yes. Often students dive right in, worried that planning will take up valuable time. But 5 minutes spent organising a well-structured answer is loads better than pages of waffle. Mmm waffles.

Writing Introductions and Conclusions

Now you've made that plan that I was banging on about on the last page, you'll know what your main points are. This is going to make writing your introduction and conclusion as easy as pie.

Get to the point straight away in your introduction

1) First, you need to work out what the question is asking you to do:

> How is the character of Jem important to the novel?
>
> The question is asking you to think about the role of Jem in the text. Plan your essay by thinking about how Jem links to the novel's key themes.

2) When you've planned your essay, you should start it by giving a clear answer to the question in a sentence or two. Use the rest of the introduction to develop this idea. Try to include the main paragraph ideas that you have listed in your plan, but save the evidence for later.
3) You could also use the introduction to give your opinion. Whatever you do, make sure your introduction makes it clear how your answer fits the question.

Your conclusion must answer the question

1) The most important thing you have to do at the end of your writing is to summarise your answer to the question.
2) It's your last chance to persuade the examiner, so make your main point again.
3) Use your last sentence to really impress the examiner — it will make your essay stand out. You could develop your own opinion of the text or highlight which of your points you thought was the most interesting.

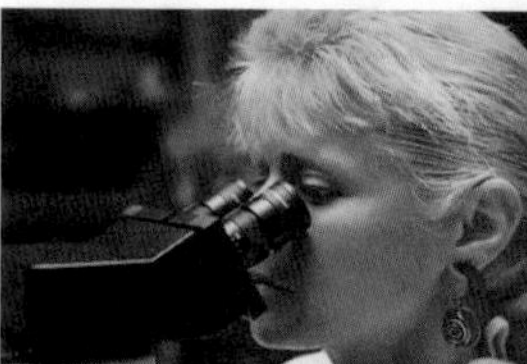

The examiner was struggling to see the answer clearly.

Use the question words in your introduction and conclusion

1) Try to use words or phrases from the question in your introduction and conclusion.

> How does Lee use symbolism in 'To Kill a Mockingbird'?

2) This will show the examiner that you're answering the question.

> Lee uses symbolism in 'To Kill a Mockingbird' to represent important themes, such as innocence, isolation and prejudice.

The first line of the introduction gives a clear answer, which will lead on to the rest of the essay.

3) This will also help you keep the question fresh in your mind so your answer doesn't wander off-topic.

I've come to the conclusion that I really like pie...

To conclude, the introduction eases the examiner in gently, whilst the conclusion is your last chance to impress. But remember — the examiner doesn't want to see any new points lurking in those closing sentences.

Writing Main Paragraphs

So we've covered the beginning and the end, now it's time for the meaty bit. The roast beef in between the prawn cocktail and the treacle tart. This page is about how to structure your paragraphs. It's quite simple...

P.E.E.D. is how to put your argument together

Remember to start a new paragraph every time you make a new point.

1) P.E.E.D. stands for: Point, Example, Explain, Develop.
2) Begin each paragraph by making a point. Then give an example from the text (either a quote or a description). Next, explain how your example backs up your point.
3) Finally, try to develop your point by writing about its effect on the reader, how it links to another part of the text or what the writer's intention is in including it.

Use short quotes to support your ideas

1) Don't just use words from the novel to show what happens in the plot...

> Jem is emotional — "When we went in the house I saw he had been crying; his face was dirty in the right places".

This just gives an example from the text without offering any explanation or analysis.

2) Instead, it's much better to use short quotes as evidence to support a point you're making.
3) It makes the essay structure clearer and smoother if most quotes are embedded in your sentences.

It's better to use short, embedded quotes as evidence. Then you can go on to explain them.

> Jem is emotional, but he tries to hide this from Scout — she notices that he's been "crying" after Mr Radley fills the tree with cement, even though she "had not heard him". Jem is sensitive, but he wants Scout to see him as brave and mature.

Get to know some literary language

1) Using literary terms in your answer will make your essay stand out — as long as you use them correctly.
2) When you're revising, think about literary terms that are relevant to the text and how you might include them in an essay. Take a look at the table below for some examples.

Literary Term	Definition	Example
Symbol	Something used by an author to represent something else.	The snowman is made of dirt covered in snow, symbolising that everyone is the same underneath.
Personification	Where objects are described using human characteristics.	The Radley house looks "droopy and sick", as if it's an ill person.
First-person narrative	Narrative written from a character's perspective, using 'I' and 'we'.	Lee uses a first-person narrative (Scout's) to create realism.

This page is so exciting — I nearly...

Now now, let's all be grown-ups and avoid the obvious joke. It's a good way of remembering how to structure your paragraphs though. Point, Example, Explain, Develop. Simple. Maybe we could make a rap or something... anyone?

In the Exam

Keeping cool in the exam can be tricky. But if you take in all the stuff on this page, you'll soon have it down to a fine art. Then you can stroll out of that exam hall with the swagger of an essay-writing master.

Don't panic if you make a mistake

1) Okay, so say you've timed the exam beautifully. Instead of putting your feet up on the desk for the last 5 minutes, it's a good idea to read through your answers and correct any mistakes...
2) If you want to get rid of a mistake, cross it out. Don't scribble it out as this can look messy. Make any corrections neatly and clearly instead of writing on top of the words you've already written.

This is the clearest way to correct a mistake. Don't be tempted to try writing on top of the original word.

3) If you've left out a word or a phrase and you've got space to add it in above the line it's missing from, write the missing bit above the line with a '^' to show exactly where it should go.

Re-read the sentence carefully to work out where the '^' symbol needs to go.

and hyperbole
The writer uses imagery ^ to draw attention to this point.

4) If you've left out whole sentences or paragraphs, write them in a separate section at the end of the essay. Put a star (*) next to both the extra writing and the place you want it to go.

Always keep an eye on the time

1) It's surprisingly easy to run out of time in exams. You've got to leave enough time to answer all the quest you're asked to do. You've also got to leave enough time to finish each essay properly — with a clear end
2) Here are some tips on how to avoid running out of time:

- Work out how much time you have for each part of your answer before you start.
- Take off a few minutes at the beginning to plan, and a few minutes at the end for your conclusion.
- Make sure you have a watch to time yourself — and keep checking it.
- Be strict with yourself — if you spend too long on one part of your answer, you may run out of time.
- If you're running out of time, keep calm, finish the point you're on and move on to your conclusion.

Stephanie never had a problem with keeping co

Treat an exam like a spa day — just relax...

Some people actually do lose the plot when they get into the exam. The trick is to keep calm and well... carry on. If you make sure you get your exam technique sorted, you'll be as relaxed as a sloth in a room full of easy chairs.

Sample Exam Question

And now the bit you've all been waiting for — a sample exam question and a lovely little plan. Go and make yourself a cup of tea, settle down and enjoy.

Here's a sample exam question

Read this feisty exam question. That's the best way to start...

Read the question carefully. Underline the important bits.

Remember to look at the book as a whole.

Q1 How is the theme of prejudice presented in *To Kill a Mockingbird*?

This gives you plenty to write about — your answer will probably be mainly about racial prejudice but for the top marks you should write about other types of prejudice too.

When you're writing your answer stick to the question. Points which have nothing to do with what you've been asked won't impress the examiner.

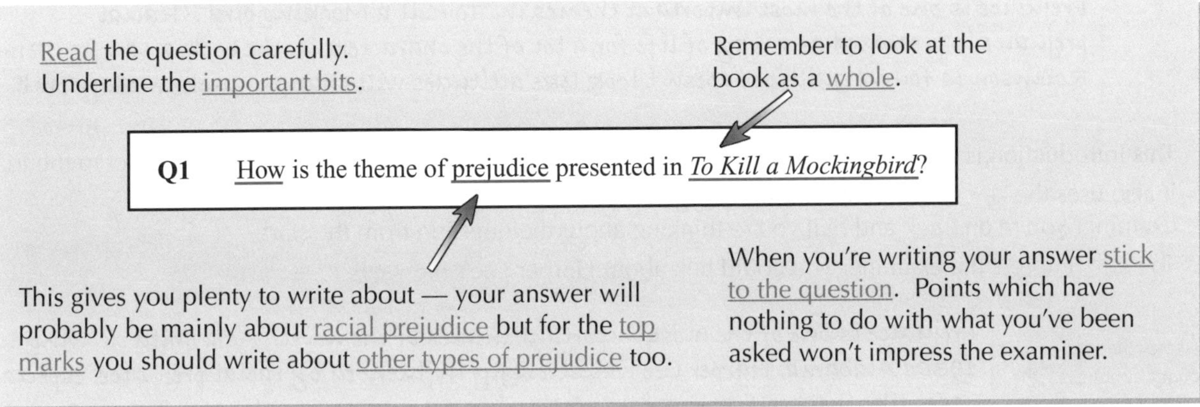

Here's how you could plan your answer...

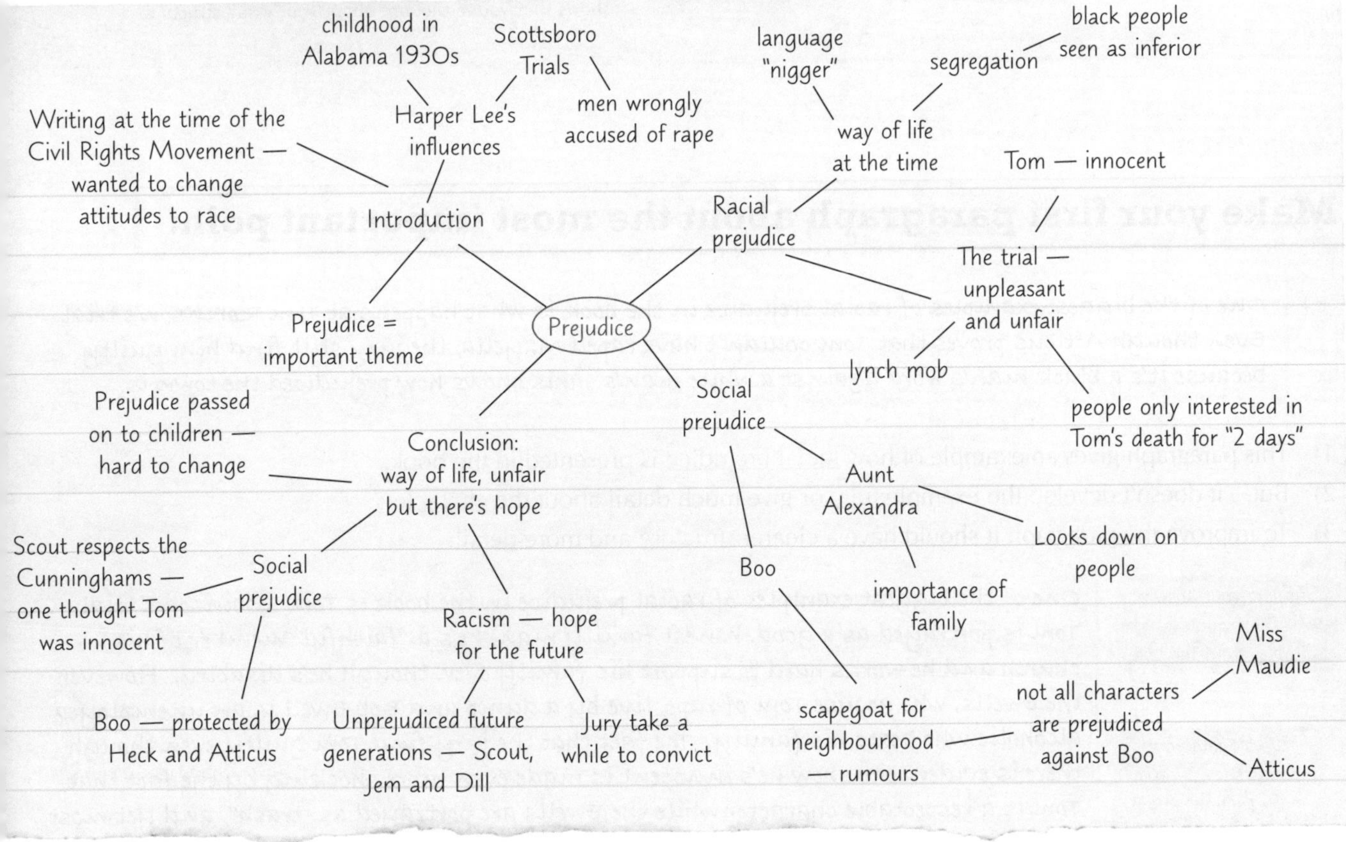

Prejudice
Introduction
Harper Lee's influences
childhood in Alabama 1930s
Scottsboro Trials
men wrongly accused of rape
Writing at the time of the Civil Rights Movement — wanted to change attitudes to race
Prejudice = important theme
Racial prejudice
way of life at the time
language "nigger"
segregation
black people seen as inferior
The trial — unpleasant and unfair
Tom — innocent
lynch mob
people only interested in Tom's death for "2 days"
Social prejudice
Aunt Alexandra
Looks down on people
importance of family
Boo
scapegoat for neighbourhood — rumours
not all characters are prejudiced against Boo
Miss Maudie
Atticus
Conclusion: way of life, unfair but there's hope
Prejudice passed on to children — hard to change
Social prejudice
Scout respects the Cunninghams — one thought Tom was innocent
Boo — protected by Heck and Atticus
Racism — hope for the future
Unprejudiced future generations — Scout, Jem and Dill
Jury take a while to convict

What do examiners eat? Why, egg-sam-wiches of course...

The most important thing to remember is not to panic. Take a deep breath, read the question, underline the key words, write a plan... take another deep breath... and start writing. Leave 5 minutes at the end to check your answer too.

Worked Answer

These pages will show you how to take an OK answer and turn it into a really good one that will impress the examiner.

Use your introduction to get off to a good start

These pages are all about how to word your sentences to impress the examiner, so we haven't included everything from the plan on page 69.

You might start with something like...

> Prejudice is one of the most important themes in 'To Kill a Mockingbird'. Racial prejudice is presented as a way of life for a lot of the characters in the book and after Tom Robinson is found guilty it doesn't look like attitudes will change much in Maycomb.

1) This introduction is okay. It mentions attitudes to prejudice at the time and how characters react to the trial.
2) It also uses the key words in the question to give the essay focus and show the examiner you're on track and that you're thinking about the question from the start.
3) To really impress the examiner you could talk about Harper Lee's message:

> Prejudice is one of the most important themes of the novel. As a child growing up in 1930s Alabama, Harper Lee was strongly influenced by racial prejudice, especially cases like the Scottsboro Trials where nine men were wrongly accused of rape because they were black. Harper Lee presents prejudice as something which is deeply unfair, but she also shows that there is hope for future generations to be less prejudiced.

This shows that you've thought about the social and historical context of the book

This tells the examiner what the essay's about and shows that you've thought about your essay structure.

Make your first paragraph about the most important point

> One of the biggest examples of racial prejudice in the book is what happens at Tom Robinson's trial. Even though Atticus proves that Tom couldn't have raped Mayella, the jury still find him guilty because it's a black man's word against a white man's. This shows how prejudiced the town is.

1) This paragraph gives an example of how racial prejudice is presented in the book.
2) But... it doesn't develop the example fully or give much detail about the characters.
3) To improve the paragraph it should have a clearer structure and more detail:

> One of the biggest examples of racial prejudice in the book is Tom Robinson's trial. Tom is portrayed as a good, honest family man, he's a "faithful" member of his church and he works hard to support his family even though he's disabled. However, the Ewells, who accuse Tom of rape, live by a dump and Bob Ewell is an unemployed alcoholic who beats his family. The fact that the jury find Tom guilty even though there is evidence to show he's innocent is made even more shocking by the fact that Tom is a respectable character while the Ewells are portrayed as "trash", and yet most of Maycomb are pleased Tom has been found guilty. This shows how for most people in Maycomb racism is part of daily life.

Support your answer with short quotes and examples from the text.

Developing your points shows you've really thought about your answer.

Referring back to the question keeps your answer focused.

Worked Answer

You need to make a variety of points

After you've explained how racial prejudice is presented you might want to start your next paragraph like this:

> The novel also explores the theme of social prejudice. Harper Lee does this by introducing the character of Boo Radley, a mysterious man who has become the town's scapegoat because he is misunderstood.

1) This introduces the idea that there are other forms of prejudice in the novel which shows a good knowledge of the text.
2) However, you can make this paragraph better by giving more detailed examples and backing up points with quotes:

> The novel also explores the theme of social prejudice through the Radley family. The Radleys are gossiped about because they don't go to church and they keep themselves to themselves showing that Maycomb is intolerant of people who behave differently. Boo Radley, the family's reclusive son, hasn't been seen for "fifteen years" but is still blamed for "any stealthy crimes" committed in Maycomb. This shows how the people of Maycomb use Boo as a scapegoat for their problems.

This shows that you have really understood the text.

Make sure you use a range of quotes, but don't quote huge chunks. Keep them snappy and relevant.

3) You could also develop it by saying how different characters react in different ways to Boo:

> But not everyone in Maycomb is affected by the same social prejudices, some characters like Miss Maudie and Atticus refuse to take part in neighbourhood gossip. Miss Maudie defends Boo by telling Scout that the rumours about him are false and that he was a polite boy, "he always spoke nicely to me".

Mentioning both sides of the point shows that you've really thought about your answer and developed it well.

Finish your essay in style

You could say:

> In conclusion, Harper Lee presents both racial and social prejudice as unfair because they are based on people's misunderstandings and fears and lead people to behave irrationally.

1) This conclusion is okay but it doesn't summarise how Harper Lee presents prejudice in *To Kill a Mockingbird*.
2) So to make it really impressive you could say something like...

> In conclusion Harper Lee presents both social and racial prejudice in 'To Kill a Mockingbird' as being part of people's way of life in small towns in 1930s Alabama. She shows how prejudices are based on fear and misunderstanding and are passed on through generations and reinforced by society and the legal system. However Harper Lee gives her readers hope by suggesting that things are starting to change at the end of the novel. The fact that Scout and Jem have learned so much from the trial suggests that they have been enlightened and that future generations may be less tolerant of prejudice. Finally, the fact that Atticus and Heck Tate try and protect Boo Radley after Bob Ewell's death shows that Harper Lee wanted to suggest that there are always people in the world who are willing to stand up to prejudice.

This focuses on the question. The word "However" shows that you're developing your answer.

Make your last sentence really stand out — it's your last opportunity to impress the examiner.

Why do alligators write good essays? Their quotes are snappy...

It seems like there's a lot to remember on these two pages, but there's not really. To summarise — write a good intro and conclusion, make a good range of points (one per paragraph) and develop your points fully with plenty of analysis.

Index

The Characters from 'To Kill a Mockingbird'

Phew! You should be an expert on *To Kill a Mockingbird* by now. But if you want a bit of light relief and a quick recap of the novel's plot, sit yourself down and read through *To Kill a Mockingbird — The Cartoon*...

Harper Lee's 'To Kill a Mockingbird'